THE DISTRICT
MORAY

MORAY has much to offer the discerning venturer. It is a landscape of dramatic change: from the desolation of the upland moors, the densely wooded hills and valleys, the fertile plains of the Laich, to the vast, windswept seascapes of the Firth.

Buildings reflect their landscape settings, as indeed they are a reflection of history. Moray is rich in both, and this guide does much to promote a deeper awareness of its heritage. However, it is more than just a record of the past; a framework is provided within which more recent achievements are placed in context. If we fail to appreciate history, we cannot contemplate the future with any confidence.

The willingness of Moray District Council, the HIDB and Messrs Chivas Brothers to contribute to the publication of this guide is gratefully acknowledged, and bears testimony to a continuing commitment to the enhancement of the built environment.

ANDREW P. K. WRIGHT
PRESIDENT, *Inverness Architectural Association*

© *Author and series editor: Charles McKean*
Series consultant: David Walker
Cover design: Dorothy Steedman
Interior and production: Charles McKean

Scottish Academic Press
Royal Incorporation of Architects in Scotland
ISBN 0 7073 0528 4
1st edition November 1987

Cover illustrations: The Laich of Moray photographed by Charles McKean; inset with paintings by Emma Black of Pann's Port and Lossiemouth, photographed by White House Photography.

Printed by Lindsay & Co. Ltd., Edinburgh

E. Black
Coxton Tower

To many people, their introduction to, and their sole experience of, Moray is the weary road from Aberdeen to Inverness. Thus has it been for centuries. *Moray loons* knew better, and were content to let travellers pass on. Wise Moravian nabobs returned from their overseas service to this mellow spot clutching their piles, with which they built or altered other piles in which to retire. The climate was as equable as could be found in Scotland.

The purpose of this volume is to persuade readers to stop in Moray or, even better, to venture a special visit. If they derive even only a tithe of the pleasure that Moray has given the author during its preparation, they will be well requited — and will return.

This magical district runs from Brodie east to Cullen and south to the Cabrach and the Lecht. It comprises most of the old county of Moray and much of that of Banff, and offers a microcosm of Scotland: rich lowland farming in the Laich, a necklace of cliffs, crags and fishing villages to the east, the uplands of Dallas and Keith, and the highlands of Glenlivet and Strathavon to the south. It is one of Moray's many paradoxes that its highlands lie to the south and not — as for the rest of Scotland — to the north. All it lacks to be a complete microcosm is an industrial city.

Enchanted ruins of great beauty testify to the importance and attraction of this place stretching back beyond the Dark Ages. It is thought that the promontory running from Kinnedar to Burghead was a centre of Pictland; and the pass of Grange, in which have been traced two large Roman marching camps, is one of the favoured sites for the important but enigmatic battle of *Mons Graupius* between Agricola and the Picts.

The Province of Moray, with its ruler (or Mormaer) was semi-independent until the early Middle Ages, protected from the rest of Scotland, as it was, by the natural barriers of mountain ranges and turbulent rivers. Even after the Crown asserted its authority by the implantation of feudalism and the Earls of Moray over the local Thanes, and the Roman Church over the Culdees, Moray's very distance from the centre of Scotland seems to have permitted considerable autonomy. Although visits by the Crown north of the Grampians were rare, the allegiance of the rulers of Moray was always a significant factor in Scots politics. Maybe that accounts for the presence of so many great monuments: Duffus, Balvenie, Darnaway, Auchindoun, Lochindorb, and the fragmentary Boharm, Drumin and Rothes castles; Elgin Cathedral and the ecclesiastical splendours of Kinloss, Pluscarden and Spynie palace.

A contrast of castles.
Opposite: Coxton Tower painted by Emma Black. **Below:** The grim ruins of Auchindoun Castle, home of Edom o' Gordon.

RCAHMS

White House Photography

Above: Lossiemouth and Coulard Hill by Emma Black.

Alexander Seton (1559-1622) was granted the lands of Pluscarden in 1565 by Queen Mary as a *God-bairn gift*. He qualified as a lawyer, became Lord of Session as Lord Urquhart in 1588 (one of the new Lordships of Erection created by James VI from former ecclesiastical properties) and Lord President in 1593. In 1596 he was a leading member of the eight *Octavians,* professional men appointed by the King to manage the Crown finances, and was appointed Lord Fyvie in 1598 when that duty was over. In 1605, he became Chancellor of the Realm as the Earl of Dunfermline (hence the name Dunfermline House given to Elgin Cathedral's Precentor's Manse in which he lived), which he remained till his death in 1622. He had two bouts as Lord Provost of Elgin (one simultaneous with being Provost of Edinburgh) and, in view of his building proclivities elsewhere (Pinkie House in 1613 and alterations to Fyvie Castle) — it is likely that he built the gracious south wing of that building.

Its history is dominated by the Bishops and Earls of Moray, the great Comyn family, the Gordons, the Grants and those engaging (if ruthless) upstarts, the Duff Earls of Fife — the Campbells of the east coast. These later families left tower houses and mansions, from the glory of Castle Gordon and the simplicity of Kininvie to the grandeur of Gordonstoun, Aberlour and Ballindalloch. Equally important, but less well recorded in stone, were the illicit distillers and smugglers, the caterans, MacGregors and other broken men who hid in the hills of upper Strathavon, the proscribed Catholic priests in their remote fastness at Scalan gradually gaining the courage to create new churches from the mid 18th century onwards; and the fishermen, loggers and sailors.

For all that Moray preys on the aesthetic and sentimental senses, nowhere else in Scotland is the hand of rational improving man quite so manifest. The list of planned towns and relocated villages dating from the 1750-1850 period is quite remarkable: Aberlour, Archiestown, Bishopmill, Duffus, Dufftown, Dallas, Buckie, Cullen, Keith, New Keith, Newmill, New Elgin, Lossiemouth, Branderburgh, Hopeman, Fochabers, Burghead, Portgordon, Rothiemay and Tomintoul. Only two ancient Royal Burghs survive in anything like their original form, and it is sometimes nostalgic to visit communities like Garmouth and Dyke, where one is spared the relentless grid iron pattern, the principal square bisected by a main road and embellished with public lavatory or bus shelter.

It is also sobering to recollect that despite the

architectural wealth, much of life in this district was, until the 19th century at least, at subsistence level, dominated by wild, uncrossed rivers, poor drainage and unreformed farming practices. Our current view of Moray is undoubtedly conditioned by the reforming, improving and ambitious Victorians.

The arrival of the railways finally ended Morayshire isolation, and created a new tourist market in places like Cullen and Lossiemouth, based on golf, beaches and bracing bathing. The subsequent arrival of the car and closure of the railways has produced a shift away from the traditional holiday towns to the sporting, the activity, or the theme holiday. One can walk the Speyside way or along the innumerable lovely forest walks, fish, beach, ski in the Lecht, or go distillery hunting up the Fiddich, along the Isla or into the Spey uplands. There are farm, folk, fishing and country life museums, working factories, computerised knitwear, and interpretation centres.

To these should now be added a deviation, a pass down a side road, a pause by an ancient settlement, for the study of carved memorials or of the simple embellishments to cottages. In architectural terms, Moray is rich both in wealthy *vernacular* buildings and in formal architectural monuments of all ages save, possibly, the present, and this guide is intended to assist those who would wish to explore.

The results contained in this volume reinforce, if such reinforcement be necessary, the closeness of the relationship between architecture and human society, and how buildings represent — or should represent —

Buckie fish market, painted in 1921 by Peter Anson (courtesy of the Abbot, Sancta Maria Abbey, Nunraw).

The port of Burghead.

RCAHMS

The Shield bearing the initials *R.R.* on either side of a stag's head bearing a mitre, commemorates **Robert Reid** one-time sub-Dean at Elgin Cathedral. Reid was Abbot of Kinloss, and later Bishop of Orkney where he reorganised the Cathedral and founded the Grammar School. He was President of the Court of Session in 1549, and was sent as one of the witnesses of the marriage of Mary Queen of Scots with the Dauphin of France in 1558. He returned to Scotland with an expert in planting and grafting fruit trees. He died later that year, and left 8,000 merks with a view to endowing a college in Edinburgh, which became Edinburgh University.

aspirations beyond those of mere shelter. Architecture has always had a place in human society beyond that of pure function, and in historic Moray that importance has been celebrated with the achievement of graceful towns and wonderful buildings. The importance which the people of Moray put upon the quality of design will determine whether or not this tradition is carried forward into the future.

How to use this Guide

This guide is written as an introduction to the history and character of the District of Moray, as can be seen through its existing or demolished buildings. The concentration, therefore, is upon buildings and their design. Technical terms are illustrated in the glossary, but the approach of the guide has been to attempt to describe, not an inventory of **what** is there, but **why.** Someone who dignified his doorway by adding pilasters and pediment to his porch was conveying a message about his aspirations to a wider world. This guide tries to indicate what to look for in each phase of architectural fashion and what might be interpreted from it. That might also offer clues helpful in an examination of what present day society is perpetrating.

The guide is organised as follows: beginning with Elgin, it follows a geographical sweep from the south-west at Lochindorb, round the Laich of Moray to Fochabers, and the region east of the Spey. The guide then follows the Spey up into the hills, turning south up the Avon to end at Tomintoul. Each individual entry lists the name: address: date and architect (where known) of the building in question, followed by a commentary.

Contemporary quotations are used in the text, universally printed in *italics* to convey the feeling of actual speech. A full list of sources is given at the back. However, because frequent reference to a major source is tedious, it is mentioned here. All quotations which have no other reference are taken from the *Survey of the Province of Moray* published in 1798 by Isaac Forsyth of Elgin, and generally known as the *Muckle Isaac* (to distinguish it from a shorter version which he issued).

The numbers in the text relate to the maps on pages 172, 173 and inside front cover. Those in the index are page numbers.

Access

Many of the buildings described in this Guide are open to the public or visible from a public road or footpath. Some are private, and readers are requested to respect the occupiers' privacy.

McKean

ELGIN

As capital of the Province of Moray, cathedral city, county town and heart of the diocese, Elgin has always been favoured. Its situation is fertile, site well-watered, and climate genial. It was protected from strife-torn central Scotland by the Cairngorms to the south and, until the 19th century, by two savage, unpredictably crossable and unbridged rivers: the Spey to the east, and Findhorn to the west.

Although the name *Helgyn* on the town's seal may imply Norse links, recorded history only begins with King David I who referred to *my burgh of Elgin* in 1150. In 1224, Pope Honorarius agreed to the removal of the Cathedral of Moray from its third resting place at Spynie (see p. 105) to its final site by the Holy Trinity Church, which lay just outside the burgh's eastern boundary on the haughs of the Lossie. Around the Cathedral grew up its own walled city, known as the Chanonry, which abutted with the town at the Little Cross.

Of the *good town* visited by King Edward I (Hammer of the Scots) in 1296, only the plan survives intact: a town stretched like an elongated tear-drop along a ridge overlooking the Lossie flood-plain. The old Tolbooth and Parish Church, which occupied the centre of the tear, fell to 19th century improvements. The original dwellings, single-storey thatched cottages, gable-end to the street, were replaced from the 17th century onwards, as the first of Elgin's successive waves of rebuilding got under way. Growing prosperity led to 300 years of persistent redevelopment

Elgin from the east in 1843, drawn by David Alexander.

Macbeth was Mormaer (ruler) of Moray, grandson of Kenneth II, and married to Gruoch, grand-daughter of Kenneth III. He thus had as strong a right to the Scottish Crown as his second cousin Duncan. Duncan seems not to have been strong, defeated by Earl Alfred of Northumbria to the south; and twice by Jarl Thorfinn Sigurdsson to the north — once at the Pentland Firth and the other at Torness (thought to be Burghead). After the latter, Duncan was mortally wounded at Bothgowan near Elgin and died in the Castle. Macbeth became king in 1040 and ruled strongly (no evidence of internal dissent) until his death at Lumphanan at the hand of Malcolm Canmore (big head) in 1054. His son Lulach ruled for another three years until his death at the hands of Malcolm.

by burghers anxious to be up with the fashion of the time.

The late 18th century, by contrast, was a period of decline. Boswell found *a place of little trade, thinly inhabited* as he accompanied Dr Johnson; whereas the latter encountered (so he wrote) the only poor meal he received in Scotland. A scarcely believable local tale attributes this immortalised disaster to Mine Host mistaking the orotund Doctor for a regular similarly orotund, whose preferred diet was alcohol in solitary splendour. In 1784, Col. Thomas Thornton thought that Elgin *in filthiness exceeded all the town of the north-east*, and as late as 1819, Robert Southey, Poet Laureate, could still be disconcerted by the *appearance of decay . . . and an abominable drum . . . beaten at nine.*

Yet improvements were on their way. Between 1820 and 1840, Elgin was transformed into a stately neo-classical town, much of which survives today. It contained all the necessary institutions, was building a handsome suburb to the south, and was surrounded by elegant villas dotted amidst trees.

Society, particularly Nabobs from India, had returned. By 1838, the town had become upwardly

Below: 17th century arcaded buildings in the High Street: Nos. 42-46 and 50-52.
Below right: Elgin from the air, the Little Cross at the top right, and Cooper Park top left.

The late 17th and early 18th centuries were good to Elgin, and Daniel Defoe visited it at a high point: *as the country is rich and pleasant, so here are a great many rich inhabitants, and in the town of Elgin in particular; for the gentlemen, as if this was Edinburgh or the Court for this part of the island, leave their Highland habitations in winter and come and live for the diversion of the place, and plenty of provisions; and there is, on this account, a great variety of gentlemen for society. This makes Elgin a very agreeable place to live in.*

mobile, *much resorted to by families in easy and affluent circumstances who find in Elgin most of those rational pleasures and advantages which attend a residence in the Capital.* Its new buildings reflected its aspirations, and included *an excellent Academy, extensive public library, a well-conducted weekly print, and a richly endowed institution for the support of old people.*

Elgin lost that sense of status once Scottish affairs became concentrated within the central belt. Its burghers quit the historic core, which rotted, for new suburbs which blurred its edges. The mid 20th century was unkind to it.

Its position straddling the great north road from London to Inverness made it vulnerable to increasing traffic, and the pressure to demolish anything that impeded it. From the south, came the impetus for Sixties' chain store developments, which treated Elgin with scant respect. The town centre by-pass, Alexandra Road, swept so close to the core as to cause dislocation between Chanonry and town, the severing of North Street (with its planned vista) and a haemorrhaging of the former tight sense of enclosure. Ten years on, some of the older lanes and wynds have been restored or rebuilt, and some excellent conservation has been attempted. Elgin is just in time to rediscover its identity.

Above: High Street c. 1895.

Writing in 1860, the celebrated historian Cosmo Innes expressed his dislike of Elgin's habit of keeping up with fashion at the expense of antiquity. *I cannot but feel some indignation at the vulgar modernising which Elgin has undergone in our time. The irregular tall houses standing on massive pillars and arcades, the roofs of mellow grey stone broken picturesquely with frequent windows, the tall crowstepped gables, are poorly exchanged for the prim and trim square modern houses and shops.*

Below: Central Elgin from the north, showing the High Street on its ridge and the closes descending from it.

Top: The western towers.
Above: The Chapter House from across the Lossie.

¹ **Elgin Cathedral** from 13th century

My church was the ornament of the realm, the glory of the kingdom, the delight of foreigners and stranger quests: an object of praise in foreign realms. Thus the lament of Bishop Alexander Bur to King Robert III after the Cathedral's sack by the Wolf of Badenoch in June 1390.

The Cathedral was consecrated on this site in 1224 by the Bishop of Caithness, and it is clear from the care, money and masoncraft which was lavished upon it — more than upon any other comparable Scots building — that this time the Cathedral was going to stay. Its removal from Spynie bears similarities to the removal from Old Sarum to Salisbury, and its setting, on flat lands bounded by a river overlooked by a ridge, is comparable to Norwich.

The **West Front,** unique amongst Scots religious buildings of that period, is framed by two identical towers. Between them are the remains of the great west window (note how it did not quite fit). Below that is the Cathedral's glory: the great west door. It is a processional doorway, French in influence, split by a central column. The oval panel above that column, surrounded by intricate carvings of angels, was designed to hold a carving of the Holy Trinity. Above that, is a row of three damaged, highly ornamental, spurious gables, with trefoil carvings.

The **Nave** is almost entirely lost, although its proportions may be inferred by studying the inside of the western front. Its unusual feature was the double-aisle, the outer of which consisted of a series of gabled chapels, rather like those which 18th century engravings show used to exist in St Giles', Edinburgh. The windows of two of those chapels, with their rich 15th century tracery, survive on the south side. Only the outer walls of the **Transepts** survived the collapse of the central tower in 1711, and they display early characteristics. The northern contains two effigies, and the south two richly carved tomb recesses.

The **Choir and Presbytery** must have glowed, so many are the windows which illuminated them. The east gable is a splendid composition of a rose window supported by two tiers of five broad lancet windows, and the side walls are lit by rows of delicately carved lancet windows at clerestorey level. Walls separated the Choir from the aisles on either side. St Mary's aisle, to the south, is still vaulted, and contains fine sculpted tombs, the most splendid being that of Bishop John Winchester, c. 1460.

The octagonal **Chapter House** is reached through a vestibule from the north aisle. It owes its survival to its use after the Reformation by the Incorporated Trades, and its fine window tracery to Historic

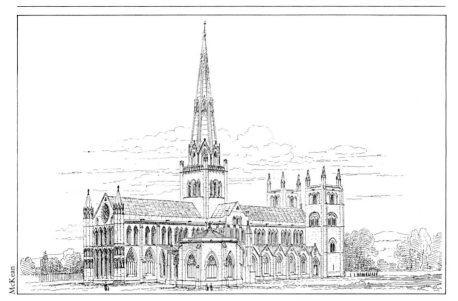

McKean

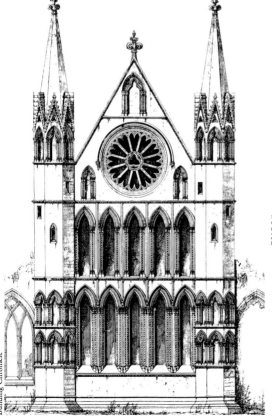

Building Chronicle

RIAS Library

The Cathedral as people have imagined it:
Top: The north front by David Alexander in 1843.
Above: The west front by John Grant, c. 1830.
Left: The east front by J. J. Laing, drawn in 1847.

Monuments, SDD, who have just completed its restoration. The splendid ribbed vaulting was added c. 1482-1501, and springs from a central pillar. It is enlivened by carvings of demons, foxes and dwarfs. Open to the public. Guide book available.

The Cathedral had an eventful life. Barely 20 years after its foundation, it was damaged in a serious fire. In 1390 it was attacked by Alexander Stewart, Wolf of Badenoch, who surged out of his stronghold at Lochindorb (see p. 49) in revenge against the sentence of excommunication passed against him by the Bishop for his tyrannical ways. He burnt Forres, and moved on to Elgin in June. The Cathedral was set alight with a thoroughness that required so substantial a rebuilding that the Chapter agreed that whomsoever should be elected Bishop in future, would have to devote one third of his revenues toward the cost, until complete. The original west window, nave arcades, crossing and Chapter House were all casualties.

In 1402, the Chanonry was *spulzied* by Alexander Macdonald of the Isles, who returned a second time that year for more, only to find Bishop and Chapter ready to outface him. In 1506, part of the great central tower collapsed and was rebuilt with huge florid statues. In 1555, the Innes clan decided to tangle with the Dunbars at what became known as the *bloody vespers*, in the Cathedral: yet, all that is recorded of a pitched battle between almost 200 people, are *several hurtings*.

The Cathedral died of neglect after the Reformation in 1560. Its last bishop, the infamous Patrick Hepburn, had alienated to him and his kin most of the lands and estates that paid for the Cathedral's upkeep, and he retired unmolested and comfortable to his great palace at Spynie (see p. 104) where he died thirteen years later. In 1567, the Regent Earl of Moray instructed the removal of the lead from the Cathedral roof to help pay his army. *I hope* commented Dr Johnson two centuries later *that every reader will rejoice that this cargo of sacrilege was lost at sea.*

In 1594, a surprise Mass was once more celebrated in the Cathedral, part roofless though it must have been, when the Catholic Earls of Huntly and Errol came to celebrate their victory over the infidel Earl of Argyll at Glenlivet (see p. 165). It was a false dawn. The decay continued. In 1599, the Kirk Session forbade using the ground for *all profane pastyme . . . and specially futballing through the toun, snow balling, singing of carrelles or other profane songis, guysing, pyping, violing and dansing. . . . All women and lassis forbidden to haunt or resort . . . in the Chanonrie Kirk*

McKean

McKean

RIAS Collection

Chalmers

Top: The Cathedral drawn in 1672 by Captain John Slezer.
Above left: The west front.
Right: The Choir arcades.
Left: The Choir.

OPPOSITE: The Chapter House, and two of its restored windows.

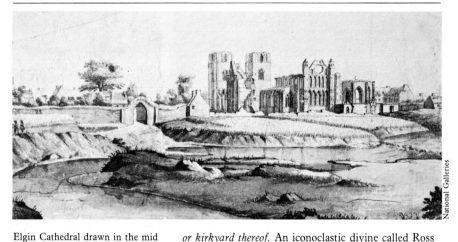

Elgin Cathedral drawn in the mid 18th century by Paul Sandby. Note the unrestored Pann's Port, the Chanonry wall, and North College to the right of the Chapter house.

OPPOSITE
Top: The Bishop's Palace, restoration as proposed by J. J. Isaac, c. 1900. **Middle:** Unthank Manse in 1843 by D. Alexander. **Bottom:** King Street.

The Cathedral and kirkyard contain splendid 16th-18th century monuments and tombs commemorating both noble families (the Earls of Gordon, the Dunbars, Innes etc.) and burgesses and members of the Trades. They are well represented by that of John Geddes, glover, and his spouse Issobell McKean. Carved in 1687, it enlightens us thus:

> This World is a City
> Full of Streets;
> And death is the Mercat
> That all men meets.
> If life were a thing
> That money could buy;
> The poor could not live
> And the rich would not die.

or kirkyard thereof. An iconoclastic divine called Ross achieved malignant immortality for the destruction of the painted rood screen in 1640. The collapse of the mid tower in 1711 took the entire nave and the roof of the choir as well, and it was not until 1807 that the Government accepted responsibility for the ruins.

The Chanonry (or College)
The Bishop of Moray was king in his own city; and, being one of the most powerful prelates in Scotland, had the Chanonry enclosed with a wall 3.7 m. (12 ft.) high, 2 m. (6½ ft.) thick, and over half a mile in circuit. It had four gates, of which **Pann's Port** is the sole survivor. Restored in 1857, this gateway is picturesquely mediaeval but cannot look anything like its original appearance, since it would have to have been at least a storey higher to accommodate the machinery for lifting its portcullis (for which the groove or *chase* still remains). Its broad shouldered, pointed Gothic arch, built of beautifully cut stone, is flanked by arrowloops and capped by a square-headed pediment.

This walled city enclosed much of Cooper Park, North and South College Streets, King Street and Cathedral Road, and within it lived the officers of the Cathedral as in a Close. They comprised 8 Dignitaries (e.g. Dean, Precentor, Chancellor, etc.), 16 Canons, 22 Vicars Choral, and a similar number of Chaplains — many of whom had livings elsewhere in the Diocese (e.g. Duffus). Several of their manses survived to an hundred years ago, and three — the so-called Palace, the North and the South Colleges — still do to some degree.

The **Bishop's Palace** dates back to 1406, and was probably built as the Precentor's House. We are now looking at a rump of a rump: much was demolished in 1851, and the spacious south wing, with its decorative

RCAHMS

McKean

oriel window, collapsed 40 years later. What survives is the ground floor, above cellars, of that wing, some garden wall, and a tall, narrow tower entered up a square stairtower against the south gable. Note the many heraldic panels, and how each crowstep is formed like a miniature gable, one with three heads.

4   The L-plan **North College** was probably built as the Deanery in 1520. It is a fairly substantial building for that time, with good mouldings, corbels and pedimented dormer windows. It was transformed in 1858 into an elegant, modernised house, a large curved bow being added between the wings. The

John Shanks, a drouthy cobbler, was appointed as second custodian of the ruins in 1824; *A thin, lank, spider-looking being in obsolete costume with a quiet earnest enthusiasm in his manner — a sort of Old Mortality whose delight it was to labour among the ruins.* To his patrons' surprise, Shanks tackled the task with enthusiasm, removing some 3,000 barrowloads of rubbish, and possibly valuable glass, timber and stone relics which, he told Lord Cockburn *made an auld man o' me.* He was quoted thus in the local paper: *Look at that floor Sir, noo as smooth's the plainstanes, an' that foundations o' the pillars therewa a' along there that I discovert wi' my ain han.* It was Shanks' excavation which revealed the elegant flight of steps leading up to the West Door. He supplemented his income by guiding visitors.

He died in 1841. Cockburn fulminated: *I was sorry to find one grave marked by an insignificant flat stone containing only the four words* John Shanks, shoemaker, Elgin. *So patient and successful an Old Mortality deserved a fuller epitaph, and I said something to induce the Elginites to give him one.* The resulting tombstone, now built into the east wall, was composed by Cockburn himself, ending: *whoso reverences the Cathedral will respect the memory of this man.*

McKean

Moray Planning Dept

Above: North College Lodge.
Right: 1 King Street.
Below right: Grant Lodge.

South College probably incorporates part of the 16th century Archdeacon's house, but its interest really subsists in its boundary wall, with its ancient arched entrance and other walled-up doorways.

King Street, the site of many of the old manses, now looks like a pretty, early 19th century, stone suburb, some of whose houses, e.g. **no. 10**, are ennobled by pilastered doorways and cornices.

The General Election in 1820 was contested by General Duff (representing the Earl of Fife) and Archibald Farquharson (in the Seafield and Kintore interest). The voters were the members of the Town Council, and feelings ran high. The Grant (Seafield) faction tried to kidnap two pro-Duff councillors, and in retaliation the Duffs carried off two of the Grant party to Sutherland. Lady Anne Grant, staying at the Seafield town house, Grant Lodge, wrote to Strathspey requesting a guard of Highlanders for protection. Three hundred men from Cromdale marched for Elgin immediately, summoning others to follow. Their passage through Aberlour was spotted by a Duff tenant who sent warning to the Elgin townsfolk who were armed and ready by the time the Highlanders marched round the town to relieve Grant Lodge. The following day armed Duff tenants continued to pour into Elgin. A battle between some 1,500 armed men was only avoided by the Sheriff persuading Lady Grant to agree to the swearing in of special constables and the dispatch of the Highlanders and others back home. By the casting vote of the Lord Provost, the Duff faction won.

5 **Grant Lodge** from 1750
Cooper Park and Elgin's Library comprise the former Grant Lodge and its policies, an ancient property of the Earls of Seafield donated to the town by Sir George Cooper in 1903. The house has the prominent cornice, pavilion roof and tall chimney stacks typical of the earlier 18th century Scottish house. It was refashioned by the Seafields with the addition of bay windows, a balustraded entrance bay, and a Doric columned portico. The local history collection within is excellent. **Lodges,** with decorative bargeboarding, were added at the same time. Cooper Park itself was laid out by A. Marshall Mackenzie, Sir George's

brother-in-law. It contains a boating pool, tennis courts, bowling green, a children's playground, and splendid views of the west front of the Cathedral. The **Eastern Entrance** to Elgin was along East Road into South College Street, the East Gate being located by the Bede House (rebuilt in the 1970s). It still begins well with a row of decent stone Council houses facing Anderson's Institution, but beyond that, the former sense of enclosure as one neared the site of the old gate has been shattered by the new road and roundabouts. The sense of *entrance* needs to be regained.

McKean

Building Chronicle

McKean

6 **Anderson's Institution,** Archibald Simpson, 1830-33
The *Elgin Institution for the support of Old Age and Education of Youth* (as inscribed above the entrance) was founded by General Andrew Anderson whose elderly mother had been left destitute and who had never been given an education. When first complete, the building comprised a school, accommodation for 50 children, and succour for ten old people. The site chosen was as an eastern sentinel to Elgin.

Top: Mid '50s houses, East Road, by Charles Doig jun.
Left and above: Anderson's Institution.

The Aberdeen architect Archibald Simpson (see **Aberdeen** in this series) was already working on the new church, and could be relied upon to produce something fittingly grand and austere. He devised a massive, two-storeyed, horizontally-proportioned H-plan building to accommodate the various uses, and minimised its bulk by projecting the two wings on either side of the entrance, each crowned by a plain pediment. Two small bays on the side elevation likewise project, a Doric portico between. The main entrance is beneath a giant Ionic colonnade, surmounted by a statue. The composition is capped by a curious, domed, circular bell-tower.

The brilliant white, Art-Deco **Elgin Motors** now acts as sentinel to South College Street. Note its shallow pediment, bay windows and flagpole. The black and white **no. 3** just opposite, dates from 1784.

Elgin Motors.

RCAHMS

The Little Cross.

McKean

7 The **Little Cross** marks the boundary between the town and the Chanonry. The rudely carved Ionic capitals supported on a circular shaft, the stepped plinth, and the sundial all date from a 1733 rebuilding; but the **finial** with its carved faces may date from the first cross of 1402, allegedly caused to be erected by Alexander Macdonald in expiation of sacrilege. It was here that his second attempt to despoil the Cathedral in the same year was outfaced by the massed dignity of Bishop and Chapter. The Victorian facade of **1 North College Street** which forms the east flank is a curious hybrid: the shallow-pitched roof which descends behind a parapet has floridly crow-stepped gables, whereas the facade below is Italianate classical: a rusticated plinth, round-headed windows on the ground floor signifying the less important rooms, and a row of dignified windows linked by a lacy balcony indicating the principal storey.

Elgin Museum, 1 High Street, 1842, Thomas Mackenzie

Below: Elgin Museum.
Right: 1 North College Street.

The Museum is a built embodiment of Elgin's *capital of the north* aspirations, founded as it was by the Elgin

Moray Planning Dept

RCAHMS

and Morayshire Literary and Scientific Association. The 26 gentlemen who founded the Association doubtless regarded it as the key activity which lifted Elgin above the run of provincial towns. Its architecture fits: cosmopolitan-Italianate in style, with the didactic overtones appropriate to a learned society. It is signalled by its tall, pyramid-roof tower and pretty group of chimneys. The broad-eaved gable alongside, with its three, tall round-headed windows indicate the galleried exhibition hall within. The growing collection required two extensions in 1896 and 1921, designed by A. Marshall Mackenzie, the son of the original architect.

8 **The Muckle Cross,** 1630, recreated by Sydney Mitchell, 1887
The heart of the original town was at the Cross, where proclamations were made, labour hired, and goods transacted. It was first erected in the cemetery surrounding St Giles, and both, impeding growing traffic, were removed in 1792. (Today, traffic undoubtedly thunders over *them bones, them bones*.) In 1887, the original Lion Rampant of 1630 was retrieved and placed on a 12 ft. high granite shaft which surges from the middle of a handsome, hexagonal structure, with shell niches and fluted Corinthian pilasters. Traffic, pedestrian barriers, flowering cherries and bulbous floodlights all contrive to diminish the considerable dignity and interest of this fine monument. On the other side of the church, facing the entrance, is a florid, three-tier wedding cake structure designed as a **fountain** by Thomas Mackenzie in 1844, but now used as an high-rise planter. The bronze lady on a circular pedestal was conceived as a **war memorial** by Percy Portsmouth in 1920.

Elgin roofscape.

McKean

The old Gaol of Elgin looked not unlike that of Forres, dominating the Market Place with its massive four-storey tower, whose peculiarly tapered stairtower projected from one corner. The courthouse alongside was a tall, three-storey crowstepped building, 17th century in character, distinguished by its later Venetian window and splendidly carved staircase. Such picturesqueness sat ill in neo-classical Elgin, and required something more *rational*.

Right: Elgin High Street in 1820.
Below: The *Muckle Kirk*.
Bottom: The Old Gaol and court-house. Compare with the opposite page to see how the town wished to move from couthiness to classicism.

The demolition of the *Muckle Kirk* (or old St Giles) caused a deep rift in Elgin society. Sentiment and long tradition argued for its repair: after all, it was buttressed, aisled, a tower above the crossing, contained good quality doors windows and pews, and had an exceptional 16th century west window. But the Choir had long gone, the nave was cramped, ill-lit and crumbling, and the original roof had been replaced by a continuous roof over nave and aisles (as had Brechin). Had it not been quite so ruinous, or had it survived until the revivalism of the 1840s, the old church would have been with us now. A mute survivor of its interior is its splendid pulpit, which survives in St Columba's (see p. 37). Even from today's perspective, the balance of benefit between the retention of the Gothic and the construction of the Grecian is difficult to evaluate.

McKean

Moray District Council

⁹**St Giles Church,** Archibald Simpson, 1825-28
The fact that the outstanding church of the Greek
Revival in Scotland was built here in Elgin is proof, if
proof were needed, of the town's early 19th century
confidence. In other towns, they repaired and
gothicised their old kirks: in Elgin, they removed the
old *Muckle Kirk* and replaced it with the purest of
ultra-modern: austere Greek from that austere Grecian
architect, Simpson of Aberdeen.

It is a subtle and elegant building. One can note
how the entrance facade facing the market place at its
broadest, is made to seem broad and low by its
pedimented temple-front, supported on six massive
Doric columns. The impression of horizontality is
reinforced by the plain frieze of laurel wreaths. It
appears to fill the eastern end of the market place. Go
round the back, however, where the market place
narrows, and an utterly different impression is created,
almost that of a different building: tall, slender, and
graceful, culminating in the round spire reaching for
the sky. Yet both facades are identical in width.

Ornament is used sparingly: only pilasters, laurel
wreaths in the frieze, and *greek-key* incised decoration
within the windows and on the principal doors. That
austerity controls the inside also. Giant pilasters surge
up the inside of the eastern wall, and the *greek-key*
motif reappears on the gallery. The panelled **pulpit,**
standing on a Doric column, beneath a dome
supported on Corinthian columns, came here in 1981
from the near contemporary Newington Parish
Church, Edinburgh, when the latter was converted
into the Queen's Hall (see **Edinburgh** in this series).

Elgin's principal landmark, however, is the spire,
mercifully still managing to tower above the

McKean

Top left: St Giles Kirk and Elgin
High Street.
Top: *New design for the tower,*
1826.
Above: The tower as built, the
restored Muckle Cross in front.

21

The Duke of Gordon Monument crowning the Castle Hill of Elgin (now Ladyhill)

The Tower, as baronialised in 1876. See opposite, top, for its appearance in 1850.

The Tower was where Isaac Forsyth founded his circulating library in 1789. It was the first such Library in northern Scotland. Forsyth (1768-1859) was also the founder of the Morayshire Farmer Club, prominent in several charities, an antiquarian and considerable publisher. He was responsible for that valuable source book **Survey of the Province of Moray,** published in 1798 and nicknamed the **Muckle Isaac** to distinguish it from an abbreviated brother.

surrounding buildings. It is a representation of that totem for classical architects: the monument erected by the ancient Greek Lysicrates, in honour of his success in a choral competition (hence the term *choragic monument*). It seemed to exemplify the purest Greek, spirit in the simplest of structures.

10 **Elgin Castle,** Ladyhill

Although this was a royal castle, allegedly that within which King Duncan died of wounds inflicted by Macbeth and one which Edward I found a *good castle* when he occupied it for four days in 1296, it figures little in history. There is some evidence that the chapel may have been rebuilt in the 15th century and lasted longer than the castle (hence Ladyhill); but it seems probable that visiting royalty and King's officials would have stayed in the palace known as Thunderton House from the 15th century onwards. Only a few lime-mortared walls, and the commanding views survive. The most notable feature now is the 1839 **Duke of Gordon Monument,** an 80 ft. high Doric column surmounted by a later statue of the 5th (and last) Duke of Gordon by Thomas Goodwillie.

High Street

The oldest building surviving in the High Street is 11 **The Tower,** although now much overwhelmed by Dr Mackay's turreted, baronial *improvements* of 1876. It represents an aristocratic town house of an older generation than the arcaded buildings, of which the haunted Calder House (removed for the building of North Street) was another. Built by Alexander Leslie, (an Elgin bailie in 1631), whose armorial panel it bears, it consisted of a two-storeyed block, principal room on the first floor, with a circular stairtower projecting into the street — a form of building not uncommon elsewhere in important 16th/17th burghs (see **Stirling** and **Dundee** in this series). The top of this stairtower is corbelled into a square, like those of Ballindalloch (see p. 163), and a lone, carved dormer windows head pokes above the roofline, searching for its long-lost window.

The Arcades

Late 17th century prosperity brought a new building form to Elgin, a cousin of one that had already been prominent in Glasgow and Edinburgh: the arcaded shop, with living quarters above. These were once so prevalent, that James Boswell could record in 1773 that there was *sometimes a walk for a considerable length under a cloister, which is now frequently broken because the new houses have another form, but seems to have been uniformly continued in the old city.* There is

McKean

Top: The Tower and its (now demolished) arcaded neighbour drawn by R. W. Billings. The design of the columns and dormer windows was unusually sophisticated.

William Duff of Dipple and Braco lived in the town house of the Coxtons of Innes from 1703-1722, and banked in the building that bears his name. He and his brother Alexander descended from Alexander of Keithmore (whose florid tomb may be seen in Mortlach Church, p. 148), and profitted from lending money on estates at a time of poor harvests, the Darien Scheme and Jacobite forfeiture, by taking possession of the property that had been advanced as security. Thus Alexander acquired Braco, and then the estate of Balvenie from the Forbes family in 1687. Alexander's son, William of Braco, was suspected of Jacobite sympathies in the '15 and, more martial than commercial, served abroad. William of Braco committed suicide in 1718 and his uncle, comfortable in Elgin, inherited his estate and continued his acquisitions. His reputation was such that the Earl of Kintore was said to pray: *Lord, keep the Hill of Foudlin between me and Braco.* Of him, but more likely of his son, also William, it was said that his boast was to concentrate all activity in the region into his hands so that *the reek o' the hale countryside cam' a' oot at a'e lum.* William III became Lord Braco in 1735 and the Earl of Fife (in the Irish Peerage) in 1759. In 1724 he commissioned James Gibbs to design a fine new mansion at Balvenie (see p. 147) and in 1735 William Adam to design Duff House, Banff. Duff House proved to be a fraught project, and Braco (as he then was) stayed in Balvenie. His son, in an attempt to prove long lineage, seized upon the Duffs of Muldavit as a suitable progenitor, and removed one of their ancient tombs to Duff House.

some doubt whether those arcades were ever quite as continuous as Boswell thought, but the habit which he noted of breaking the old pattern, is what has always happened in Elgin. The burghers consistently chose the fashionable building form of the day.

The surviving arcades are to be found at the eastern end of town, and date mainly from 1688-1694. Nos. 12 **50-52** (Master and Miss) was built by Andrew Ogilvy and Janet Hay, and is dated 1694 on the skew. Recently restored by Ashley Bartlam Partnership, it stands two-storey and attic above a muscular arcade, the arches springing from rudimentary Ionic capitals. **Shepherd's Close,** behind, is contemporary.

No. **42-46** (once the Red Lion Hotel, and thought to be the location of Dr Johnson's poor meal) is dated 1688. The central of its five massive arches leads to a pend at the rear.

The finest survivor of these, however, is **Braco's** 13 **Banking House,** facing the Little Cross. Built in 1684 by John Duncan and Margaret Innes (whose date

McKean

Left: Braco's Banking House.

and monograms decorate the superbly carved heads to the dormer windows) it is only three bays long and a storey lower. Note how the dormer head with the man's initials (I.D.) is capped with a thistle, whilst that of the lady (M.I.) has a fleur-de-lys.

The eastern High Street.

By the next phase of High Street rebuilding, arcades had clearly become *passé*, no matter how civilised they had been. The early 18th century nos. **17-27** (the first group to be restored by the Elgin Restoration Fund) are stone fronted, with regular ranks of windows and roofs of shallower pitch. No. **17-19** is dignified by an unlettered Venetian window at first floor suitable for its use as a Freemason's Lodge (hence *Masonic Close* to the rear), whereas nos. **21-23** have well-carved scrolled, trefoiled dormer window heads. The only other survivor of this period is concealed behind the later front of the **White Horse Inn,** gable to the other end of the High Street.

Shepherd's Close.

The **Closes, Wynds and Alleys,** where they survive, are now mostly of late 18th-mid 19th century, although older date and marriage stones are frequently re-used. Several have been restored by the Ashley Bartlam Partnership. All the windows and doors **face east,** the buildings are usually much lower and much more rustic than those facing the High Street, and there is only the rare exception of a polished stone facade, a porch or a fanlight. However, the Close behind no. **114,** dated 1766, was once the site of the Harrow Inn, and is paved all the way through to South Street. Note the marriage stones dated 1620 and 1725.

The expansive years: 1820-1880
The expansive years brought to Elgin new roads and vistas, and the public buildings of a regional capital: a

McKean

Moray Planning Dept

Moray Planning Dept

Museum, Magistrates' Court, Assembly Rooms, and bank after bank after bank. Many of the latter have now been replaced, particular losses being William Burn's gracious 1822 **Assembly Rooms** (only a small part of that planned to be built), and David Cousin's neighbouring, palatial **North of Scotland Bank.** The tight scale of the old town was broached by the creation of Batchen Street, North Street, Commerce Street and the widening of Lossie Wynd.

The new neo-classical buildings had characteristic motifs. Beautifully cut and polished stone took the place of plain rubble walls; the entrance would be aggrandised by a lavish porch and the principal floor (the first) by pediments and architraves above the windows; and the composition would be completed by a projecting cornice with dentils (little brackets) beneath, and a parapet above. Sometimes urns, sometimes not.

High Street — north side
No. **115,** built c. 1830 as the British Linen Bank, is an early example of the type (despite its later shop front). Urns crown the parapet above the cornice, and oriel windows dignify the first floor. Buildings of similar date, showing the decent plainness (before the style became overblown) of parapets, cornice, architraved first floor windows etc. can be found at the west end between Woolworths and the cinema. **Woolworths** itself, designed by A. and W. Reid in 1856, is composed of similar elements, but rather grander with its channelled stonework and quoins.

Without doubt, the most splendid survivor is the
14 **Royal Bank,** 141-145 High Street, a late design of this type by Peddie and Kinnear in 1876. Designed in the manner of an Italianate renaissance *palazzo*, it has three grand storeys: the topmost (the smallest), shelters beneath a huge projecting cornice; the principal floor

Top left: Western High Street. Note the classical rhythm of the buildings. **Top:** Charles Close. **Above:** Forsyth's Close.

(middle) has five tall, architraved windows; the ground floor has channelled stonework and a particularly florid, pedimented entrance.

High Street — south side
There is less of the earlier period on the south side. Nos. **76-80,** c. 1830, has the characteristic architraves and cornice, whereas the 1857 former Union Bank, nos. **82-86** has sculpted shell hoods above the first-floor windows and ornate carvings above those on the second, the whole topped by a balustrade. Nos. **96-100** and nos. **114-116** are both worth studying for their variations upon the theme. Nos. **128-132** is grander, each of the seven first floor windows dignified by a semi-circular pediment, the design tied together by twin wall-head chimneys linked by a balustrade.

No. **164-166** High Street, built as the Caledonian Bank in 1845 by A. and W. Reid, is a late example. The ground floor has the customary channelled stonework and the windows on the first are emphasised in the usual manner. Note how the bays at either end project slightly and are pedimented.

Elgin Courthouse: William Robertson's elegant design for a Court and Council offices, was replaced after the War by the current District offices.
Bottom: The 1864 Sheriff Courts by Robertson's nephews, A. and W. Reid.

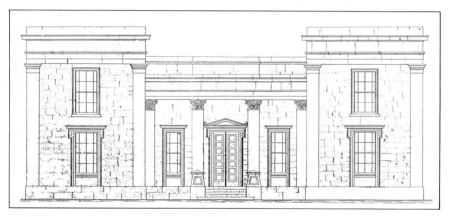

15 **Sheriff Court,** A. and W. Reid, 1864-66
Although elsewhere in Scotland such Courts were going baronial in style, neo-classicism (quite rightly) still ruled in Elgin. *More elegant than might be looked for in a city the size of Elgin* thought contemporaries. Another *palazzo,* the emphasis is placed upon the principal floor sitting above a plain lower storey with channelled stonework. That emphasis is created by pairs of Ionic columns, architraved windows with balustrades below, and corners picked out with vermiculated (worm-eaten) quoins. Remarkably unaltered inside.

PSA

McKean

Post-classicism, 1850-1914

The discipline began to break down as Victorian commercial individualism began to dominate Elgin, and the signs can be spotted as early as the new buildings by Commerce Street, of the 1850s, which introduced round-headed windows, keystones and like details. The 1880s block at no. **83** High Street has pairs of Romanesque windows in recessed bays, whilst its 1870 neighbour, nos. **85-93** is a long, exuberant block with square headed windows and string courses. **Union Buildings,** on the corner of Lossie Wynd even sports a stumpy tower on its corner. In 1894, the Perth architect Andrew Heiton replaced the pleasant laird's town house beside Braco's Banking House in obtrusive baronial (now an ex-servicemen's club). The mould now broken, the High Street was ready for whatever fashion money could buy, and rebuilding commenced.

An early victim was the douce neighbour to the 16 Tower which, in 1905, gave way to nos. **107-109,** now *General George,* and four storeys of bourgeois boasting: windows pedimented, pilastered, and round-headed, the showroom on the first floor virtually transparent. Nos. **123-133** (now Arnott's), designed as a draper's store by R. B. Pratt in 1903-04, seem taller — an optical illusion created by the use of a turreted Gothic gable rather than a pediment. The details below are curious: the broad, round-headed windows at first floor level presumably indicate a selling area whereas the smaller square windows on the floor above imply cutting rooms. Other buildings of the period with less pretension include no. **94** with its dormers and cast iron railings just across the street, and the **Palace Hotel** with its lush bay windows.

McKean

Top: Elgin from the west.
Middle: Commerce Street.
Below: Ex-Servicemen's Club.

G R M Kennedy

Edwardian Elgin.

The Elgin Club.

Little changed in the High Street between the Wars, save the continual erosion of the heritage and the construction of the **Playhouse** cinema by Alister MacDonald (the Prime Minister's son) in 1932. The County Hall was redesigned, but not actually rebuilt until after the War.

The next phase of frantic rebuilding occurred mainly 1955-75, this time in an austere, visually roofless, and sober architecture, as exemplified by the **Clydesdale Bank** and the supermarket opposite. When their first life is over, the opportunity should be taken for a re-roof and refront, which should be seized and executed with the kind of flair that Elgin encouraged between 1820 and 1850.

Commerce Street, formerly School Wynd and over-trafficked, hosts two buildings of note: the tall [17] **Elgin Club** designed by A. and W. Reid in 1868 in the approved *palazzo* style. The principal floor is indicated by large rounded windows within a square frame sitting upon a balustrade, a dentilled cornice completing the elevation. A grand hall with rich plasterwork within, an elegant stair leading to the domed billiard hall upstairs. The low **T.S.B.** adjacent by the same architects, has a roofline of flat pediment, cornice, balustrade and urns.

RCAHMS

McKean

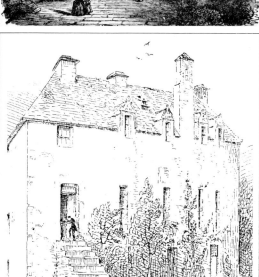

McKean

Thunderton House:
Top left: c. late 18th century,
before the removal of the tower
and the feueing of Batchen Street.
Left: In 1843. **Above:** Its
roofscape now. The chimney stack
has gone, but it otherwise remains
much as it did in 1843.

18 **Thunderton House** from 16th century
Of the *Great Lodging* of Elgin, home of the King
when passing through, and later the town house of,
successively, the Earls of Moray, Dunbars of
Westfield, and the Lords of Duffus, of this historic
pile sufficient remains for a genuine restoration to
considerable glory.

Founded in the 14th century, Thunderton grew into
a huge courtyard palace extending from its surviving
wing right down to an High Street frontage. To this,
the Sutherlands of Duffus are thought to have added a
string-coursed tower in 1650, but although the details
(and immense caryatids of savages) carried Duffus
motifs the tower was certainly much older. One can
infer from the surviving portion (with its ungainly
roof) which represents part of the north and west

Top: South Street. Note the black Art-Deco shop front alongside the New Market gateway.
Above: The Lido.

wings, some of the quality of the palace. The south facade retains four exquisitely carved dormer windows, and a flight of stairs; whereas the north (entrance) front is a jumble of re-used bits including the relics of four other dormer windows.

Elgin has always been short on sentiment. Thunderton became the property of Provosts once the aristocracy had fled to more modern piles. In 1746 it was slept in (where was not ?) by Bonnie Prince Charlie. It was rouped, and in 1801 its eastern part was feued for Batchen Street. In 1822, the tower was removed. Indeed, it is surprising that anything survives at all. Its current restoration is the latest in a long line of hostelries: but its restoration as a palace may be worthy of enquiry.

SOUTH ELGIN

South Street

The southern edge of mediaeval Elgin, now represented by South and Greyfriars Streets, was probably never walled. The rear of the buildings, the narrow entrances to the wynds, and a ditch must have provided whatever defence was needed. The track which ran along the back of that defensive edge was known as Back Lane (or Street) and here congregated the stables and the inns. The Eagle Inn, its last surviving hostelry, was replaced in 1936 by **Argyle Buildings.** The **Grand Hotel** replaced that *comfortable house,* the Royal Oak Inn, in 1898. Note the early 19th century corniced shop-window at nos. **45-47.**

The former **New Market** gateway is a painted stone *triumphal arch* erected in 1851. It has a hungry cornice, massive flat-topped pediment, and lower wings to either side. The **Picture House** was designed by Alec Cattanach in 1926: a smart, fashionable stone front, were it not for its lumpy roof and corrugated iron excrescences. The **Lido** opened the following year, on the other side of Fife Arms Close,

Highfield: The fashionable new aristocratic town house of Sir Archibald Dunbar.

to profit from the new crowds going to the pictures, and has an Art-Deco parapet, pediment and carvings. Note also the tube-like corner turret running from first floor to the roof of the 1897 **Imperial Bar.**

South Street opens up further west, beginning with Sir Archibald Dunbar's new town house, **Highfield** which was built c. 1820. This classical villa may have set the tone for many subsequent clones: entered up a flight of steps to a door flanked by Doric columns and capped by a fanlight, within a projecting, pedimented bay. The substantial **Park House Hotel** is similar. Then two churches: **High United Free,** built in the first flush of Disruption in 1843, mixes an Early English gable with lancet windows with a Romanesque door, and galleries inside. The **Free Church,** designed by a Mr Bisset 21 years later, is much purer: a tall, lancetted and buttressed box with an integral verticality that eluded many other Victorian Goths.

17 Reidhaven Street.

Reidhaven Street, looking south.

The first suburb
Elgin developed a beautiful suburb on the south-facing slopes between 1820 and 1850, the north/south axis being Moss Street (which grew in importance after the development of New Elgin and the arrival of the railway) and the east/west one Moray Street. To the east, Anderson's Institution acted as a catalyst for villas, as did Dr Gray's Hospital to the south/west.

Academy, Reidhaven and South Guildry Streets all date from 1850-66, much feued by the Earl of Seafield. **No. 36 Academy Street** is a very good villa whose doorway is pilastered and architraved as typifies this street. The single-storey stone cottages of

19**Reidhaven Street** were thought in 1914 to form the *finest residential street in the City*, with their attics, pilasters and pedimented doors. Note how each house has a precise set of details to give it dignity. The **Baptist Chapel** is a neat building of 1850, with Gothic windows and a panelled Gothic balustrade.

Moray Street starts narrow from Moss Street, broadening out as it sweeps west. Its status is that conferred by four civic monuments. The soaring, 20 rubble-built **South (U.F.) Church** was designed in first-flush Victorian Gothic by A. and W. Reid in 1853. It is redolent of muscular Christianity: buttresses, lancet windows, finials, crocketts and a great spire. It lacks its original fretwork parapet.

Top: Reidhaven Street. **Above:** The South Church. **Right:** The Town Hall (now demolished).

The 1885 **Town Hall** by A. Marshall Mackenzie, which was burnt out in 1939, was a gigantic, enthusiastically detailed Dutch-gabled barn with a four storey tower, cupola and turrets, out of place both in this suburb and on the skyline.

32

McKean

Left: The Academy.
Above: Further Education College extension.

21 The 1885 **Academy** was designed by the Reids in unmistakeable pedagogic uniform: a polished stone, pedimented temple of learning sitting on a rubble plinth, entered beneath the central portico. An extremely smart and well-scaled black and white complex has been added in the grounds, as part of the **Education College,** by G. R. M. Kennedy and Partners.

McKean

Left: Victoria school of Science and Art.
Below: 26 Hay Street.

22 The fourth monument is the American — styled **Victoria School of Science and Art** designed in 1890 by George Sutherland. It is altogether curious. The plan is a simple L-shape, a campanile and porch in the heel. But the large-scaled rubbly stonework, huge fanlit windows, finials, gargoyles and suchlike, have an *insouciance* characteristic of America rather than the British pre-occupation with truth to styles.

  Hay Street, prior to being relegated to its current status as freeway, was a grander suburb, as some surviving buildings attest. The early 19th century **Darliston** (no. 40) has the characteristic pediment, with cast-iron balcony and balustrade. No. **26,** now

Moray Planning Dept

McKean

Right: '30s flats, Hay Street.
Below: 13 Wittet Drive.

McKean

The Maison Dieu, traced from an unknown drawing by Dr Thomas Ross.

RIAS Library

the office of Wittets Ltd. (direct descendants back through J. and W. Wittet, Reid and Wittet, A. and W. Reid, of Elgin's first architect William Robertson), has Tuscan pillars, polished stone, quoins and a cornice. Across the entrance to Moray Street can be found a rare 1930s block of flats by J. and W. Wittet, a granite tower indicating entrance and staircase, the flats on either side being harled horizontally.

More villas on **Mayne Road,** the 1866 **Brae Birnie,** built for a local solicitor, showing how the classical discipline was getting somewhat overripe. Note the Tudor arch to the coachhouse of the 1839 **West-End Hotel.** The 1827 **Prospect Lodge** has the usual flight of steps leading up to a pilastered front door. The view down stone **Grant Street,** begun in 1895, is closed by Grays Hospital, and the houses are lower in the pecking order: good terraced and semi-detached Edwardian. **Wittet Drive** is mostly inter-war bungalows, many designed by J. and W. Wittet. **No. 23 13** offers a pure 1930s aesthetic (although completed after the War): flat-roofed, corner windows and a pergola, at the request of the client.

Greyfriars and the Maisondieu
Elgin's grander villas lie east of Moss Street on the lands of the Greyfriars and of the Maisondieu, an important mediaeval charitable hospital whose ruins were mostly destroyed in 1750 by *a dreadful hurricane,* and traces of which were obliterated by villa development. It is a particularly delightful part of Elgin, in which the social changes of the 19th century are reflected in the villas of the wealthy.

Greyfriars from 1470
Elgin's only surviving mediaeval religious house apart from the Cathedral, it was founded by Alexander II as a Franciscan House and relocated to this site in 1479. In 1560, it was devastated by the Earl of Huntly, and

Greyfriars in 1843.

Left: Greyfriars — the drawings by architect John Kinross for its restoration.

24 until 1895 it mouldered in bosky decay, venerable trees sprouting from its inmost recesses. The 3rd Marquess of Bute provided funds for its beautiful and careful restoration by architect John Kinross as a working Convent of Mercy, which it now is. The plain rectangular church is aisleless, lit by elegant two-light Gothic windows. Kinross provided the elegant timber-vaulted roof, the splendid Gothic rood screen (not dissimilar to that in King's College, Aberdeen (see **Aberdeen** in this series) and carved oak stalls in the Choir. Some monuments to the King family of Lesmurdie, who owned the ruins in their decay, survive in the nave. The original well survives in the centre of the pleasant stone cloisters, and traces of mediaeval painting adhere to some rafters in the refectory.

Greyfriars House on the corner of Queen Street, was built c. 1846 in extravagantly picturesque Jacobean: angular, angled chimneys, a two-storeyed gabled porch, and lovely carvings. **Institution Road,** linking the Institution to Moss Street, begins with the

Greyfriars House, Queen Street.

St Sylvester's, with *Kinrara* and *Moray Bank* to the left.

McKean

East End School designed 1830-33 by Archibald Simpson with characteristics similar to the Institution itself — plain, well built and classical. The **Lodge** has a twisted chimney. The 1840 **Friars Park** (no. 9) and 1860 **Friars House** (no. 11) are both villas by A. and W. Reid, the first L-plan Italianate, with its over-hanging bracketted roof and urn above the porch, the latter more classical with Doric portico, pilasters and quoins. **Kinrara** and **Moray Bank,** a handsome pair of well-built villas with lovely front gardens, were commissioned in 1850 from the Reids by a successful wood merchant, James Watson. A diminutive pediment caps the centre window of the upper storey. Kinrara's porch is faintly Egyptian, whereas Moray Bank's is capped with a lacy balustrade of anthemion-
25 leaf design. **St Sylvester's R.C.,** designed by Thomas Mackenzie with inspiration from Bishop James Kyle, presents a most beautiful Gothic gable facing down Duff Avenue. Note particularly the window-tracery, oculus above, and buttressed corner tower.

   Duff Avenue is possibly the best of the villa-lined streets declining southwards, and contains three
26 buildings of particular note. **The Lodge** was designed in 1898 by A. and W. Reid in the new American

McKean

The Lodge, Duff Avenue.

McKean

McKean

fashion sweeping Elgin. Note the freedom with which its uses traditional details such as the pedimented porch, which is extended asymmetrically to merge with a bay window, and the muscularly-roofed corner tower, presumably offering only a window-seat, with its array of blind bulls'-eyes. The black-and-white, angular house next door, with its huge-windowed rooms in the roof, is an intriguing modern addition to the street by G. R. M. Kennedy. **St Leonard's Hotel** designed by Elgin architect Charles Doig in the same year as the Lodge, is much more traditionally baronial — towers, gables, string-courses and bay windows — epitomising the home of a late 19th century successful solicitor.

Moss Street was the principal route down to Rothes, and is lined with two churches, secluded villas, and a few shops (**nos. 42-46** with exceptional ironwork and cast-iron Corinthian columns). The 1856 **U.F. Church** is relatively undistinguished Gothic by 27 A. and W. Reid. **St Columba's,** however, designed in 1906 as a relief to St Giles' by Peter MacGregor Chalmers, is of a different order. Its plain exterior conceals a rich interior of suspiciously High Church

Yeadon

McKean

Top left: House Duff Avenue. **Above:** St Columba's Church, and the 17th century pulpit from old St Giles. **Left:** 42-46 Moss Street.

South Villa.

RCAHMS

William Robertson (1786-1841) was possibly the north of Scotland's first native classical architect of substance. His first known work is the Manse of Grange when he was 28, and it is speculated that he may have trained with John Paterson, an Elgin architect who had moved to Edinburgh in 1789 to work with Robert Adam. His first major task was for the Earl of Seafield in the new town of Cullen (see p. 128), followed by Anderson Primary School, Forres (p. 66), the Elgin Court House, and Forres Tolbooth. He added to and extended mansions like Orton, Arndilly, Kininvie, Wester Elchies and Duffus. His finest new house is Aberlour (p. 160). He died aged 55, *known and esteemed for his talents over the whole northern district of the Country.* (See Elizabeth Beaton: **William Robertson,** 1984.)

tendencies, with soaring Romanesque arches, the capitals decorated with Celtic carvings. It also contains the splendid 1684 timber **pulpit** from the old Muckle Kirk, supported on Ionic Pilasters, its canopy above on Corinthian ones.

28 **South Villa,** 41 Moss Street, 1830
Designed by William Robertson as the town house of Mrs Grant of Elchies (two years after the pair had baronialised the now-vanished 17th century Wester Elchies), South Villa is the apotheosis of the Regency villa in Elgin: two-storeys, symmetrical under its pavilion roof, the entrance facade dominated by a semi-circular, Doric-columned porch, a lacy balcony above. Balconies decorate the projecting bay windows on both the flanking gables.

Laich Moray Hotel.

McKean

29 The suave **Laich Moray Hotel,** designed in 1853 by Thomas Mackenzie, is very cosmopolitan, conveying to those arriving by railway that Elgin was not so very different to Paddington. It is a tall, symmetrical, Italianate building whose verticality is reinforced by the design of the groups of triple windows, the dentilled cornice and the chimney stacks. The Great North of Scotland **Railway Station** opposite was designed in 1898 by P. M. Barnett. Remarkably unaltered inside (despite its use as a goods

Great North of Scotland Railway Station.

station), it awaits benevolent re-use. The **Royal Hotel** (formerly Dalehapple) was built by Lord Provost James Grant for himself in 1865, and bears his initials *J. G.* on the gates.

New Elgin.

30 **New Elgin** was founded in 1830 on the slope up to the Muir of Elgin as a working men's suburb. Streets of little stone cottages lined the hill facing north to Elgin, on either side of the Rothes road. These were followed by more substantial houses and inns and, later, by bungalows. Its pleasant sense of openness still remains. A 17th century three-stage, circular **Doocot** with rat-ledge survives in the park. One of two beautiful 1950s houses, designed in 17th century Scotstyle by John Wright, can be found on Birnie
31 Road (the other in Fleurs Place).

House by John Wright, New Elgin.

NORTH ELGIN

North Elgin is dominated by the meander of the River Lossie, as it scours out its path from west to east along the bottom of the tail end of the Quarrywood ridge. Being low-lying, it never attracted the higher-quality feues that obtained in south Elgin, being content instead with trades, workers' housing and, latterly, industry. Until 1820, the principal route ran down Lossie Wynd, across the river, and up through Bishopmill (although an even earlier route crossed the river at Deanshaugh). In 1820, the haunted Calder House on the High Street was demolished to provide a mouth for a wide, new street driving downhill, to be called **North Street.** Yet, although laid out with handsome new buildings on either side, it failed to raise the utilitarian aspects to which the former Blackfriars' property had been put (the vestiges of whose monastery had been removed some 50 years before). It, in turn, has fallen prey to **Alexandra Road,** which severs it and maroons the Episcopal

Right: Holy Trinity Church.

The Haugh.

32 **Holy Trinity Church** on the far side. The key feature of this church, designed by William Robertson in 1825, was the Gothic entrance gable, which formed a visual termination to North Street: a carefully symmetrical composition, the gable consists of a late-Gothic window, framed by finials, above a parapeted porch. **Blackfriars Guest House** next door is a characterful hybrid of classical and Italianate with Gothic windows.

Little of note survives to the west save, on former monastery lands by the banks of the Lossie, **The**
33 **Haugh.** Recently converted to a hotel by Wittets Ltd., the Haugh is an extravaganza remodelled in 1882 by William Kidner for a prominent lawyer, A. G. Allan. By staid British standards, it is fantastically exuberant, grasping any motif of any origin so long as

Elgin Town Hall.

McKean

it contributes to the fun. That was an American attribute. Kidner, (1841-1900) who also remodelled Lesmurdie (see p. 43) with a similar lack of inhibition, had returned to London from Shanghai, from whence the inspiration may derive.

Lossie Green once an important social focus for Elgin, is a parking lot. Worth noting, however, are the 1950s head office of **Scottish Malt Distillers** in plain, cubist, Thirties style; and the new **Town Hall,** a bare 1960s pavilion by Kininmonth and Spence.

Elgin from across the Lossie.

McKean

34 Bishopmill

The utilitarian, iron **Bishopmill Bridge,** 1871, is named after Elgin's second mill (others on this hardworking river including Sheriff Mills, Old Mills, Kingsmills and Newmill). Bishopmill itself is worth a detour. Laid out on an east-west grid in 1798 by the Earl of Findlater, little of its quality can be

McKean

McKean

Moray Planning Dept

Moray Planning Dept

From top: Bishopmill;
Braemoriston House; Hythe Hill.
Below: Harrison Terrace.

appreciated from Bridge Street which severed it in two. For some time its High Street ends were linked by a bridge. Mostly plain stone houses and cottages on a plateau with a wonderful view over Elgin, the buildings are unspectacular but pleasant, well exemplified in East and West **Back Streets.** The grander houses line the cliffs in the **High Street** (east and west) among which **Deansford,** built in 1860, has a four-columned portico and a timber pediment, and **Millbank,** 1846, is stylishly neo-Elizabethan with octagonal chimneys and stone finials, within a beautifully landscaped garden. **Hythe Hill** was built in 1848 by a returned nabob, and is distinguished by its great bow windows overlooking Elgin, its niches, and its ornamental boathouse.

Braemoriston House, in the road named after it, is an unusual design of two-storey pavilions, each with an Ionic colonnade, joined by a single-storey entrance block whose Ionic columned porch is linked through to the colonnades on each side. The Elizabethan-style, former **poorhouse** was situated just to the north by Balmoral Terrace. The remarkable terrace opposite

RCAHMS

was designed in 1949, in traditionally arcaded Elgin
35 style, by John Wright and named **Harrison Terrace**
after Lord Provost E. S. Harrison (client for the Bield;
see p. 48). The angular new **Church** in Lesmurdie
Road with its spiky roof and dormer windows, was
designed in 1984 by J. and W. Wittet for the Chinese
Community.

McKean

Left: Newmill.
Above: Chinese Church.

Ashley Bartlam

36 **Newmill**
Newmill was one of two mills established by
Alexander Johnston in 1797. The other was at
Deanshaugh, just upstream, whose plain classical
house could have been Johnston's. Newmill's purpose
was the manufacture of *Scotch plaids, tweeds, kerseys
and double cloth,* and it expanded quickly, given a
boost by the decision of the Morayshire Farmer Club
to purchase cloth only from Newmill. In 1856 a
foundry was added for the repair of plant; but that
developed a purpose of its own by manufacturing and
supplying reaping machines, steam engines, distillery
and mill equipment. By 1868, Newmill had become
*the most important public work in the County, employing
1-2,000 hands.*

Lesmurdie doocot.

A substantial working complex survives today,
enclosing a pretty entrance courtyard, which is
dominated by the **Mill Shop** building. Converted by
the Ashley Bartlam Partnership to its current use, the
building is self-consciously grand. Formerly entered
through the gable with its Gothic windows, the
central bay of this nine-bay, two-storey mill is gabled,
with a bellcote above, thus lending the block both
symmetry and focus. The 1818 **Newmill House,** the
proprietor's own, is a harled, dormer-windowed house,
a grandiose shell-porch fronting the entrance bay.
Garvald, adjacent, is an 1868 house eaten up by the
mill's expansion, designed with a drum tower and
fish-scale roof by H. M. S. Mackay.

RCAHMS

37 **Lesmurdie,** William Kidner, 1881
Kidner's first known exploit in Elgin was this
remodelling of the patrimony of the King family of

Lesmurdie House.

Moray Planning Dept

Thomas Mackenzie (1814-54) who died of a brain fever at the tragically young age of 40 was an architect of great distinction and style. Born in Perthshire, he moved via Dundee to Archibald Simpson's office in Aberdeen when he was 21. His move to Elgin four years later to set up practice, and to buy and extend the Regency villa of Ladyhill, implies both contacts and some wealth. His output over the next 14 years was extraordinary — even if one excludes the Aberdeen branch office which he established with James Matthews in 1844. Of his vast output, his Elgin Museum, Milne's School, Fochabers, the wildly extravagant Drummuir and glorious additions to Ballindalloch, the Caledonian Bank, Forres and Laich Moray Hotel, Elgin, may be singled out as representing the verve with which he designed. He begat an even more famous son — Alexander Marshall Mackenzie, whose work in Aberdeen, particularly the design of Marischal College, is justly acknowledged (see **Aberdeen** in this series).

Lesmurdie for the Johnstons of Newmill. He seized the unpretentious cottage on the site by the throat, and metamorphosed it into a begabled, crowstepped, towered and chimneyed confection. The nearby early 19th century octagonal **Doocot** is built of dressed stone with a pyramid roof.

WEST ELGIN

Western Elgin begins at the foot of the castle hill, where the picturesque, harled houses of **Murdoch's** 38 **Wynd,** by the District Architects department, go a long way to heal the wounds of the new roundabout. The landscaping is excellent. **War Memorial Gardens** with twin towered War Veterans' houses

Moray Architects Dept

McKean

Above: Murdoch's Wynd.
Right: Ladyhill House.

linked by a sheltered arcade were added by J. and W. Wittet in 1919. The white regency village of **Ladyhill House** was transformed in 1853 by Thomas Mackenzie into his own house, adding a *beautiful specimen of Norman Gothic architecture* to the western end, and pillars and pediments from the demolished Ritchie's Land on the High Street into a loggia. His son Marshall Mackenzie, the designer of Marischal College, was born here, and christened his Aberdeen home *Ladyhill* in homage (see **Aberdeen** volume). **Lossie Bank,** in Hill Street, is a picturesque mid-century, rambling *cottage ornee* with rustic porch and decorative ridge tiles.

Maryhill House.

39   **Maryhill,** the next large villa, comes from the hand of A. and W. Reid in 1866, when they transformed a substantial classical house into Victorian ostentation. The projecting entrance bay — balustraded and urned at both porch and roof level, is flanked by twin bay windows — balustraded and urned. Square bays, similarly topped, project from either side. Two rows of seven ornate chimneys each

View of Dr Gray's Hospital down Grant Street.

line the ridge of the pavilion roof. It is as though the Reid had studied their uncle's plan for South Villa (see p. 38) and determined to smarten it up a bit. A pretty, balustraded footbridge was built at the same time. **Pluscarden Road** is suburban. The **Grove Hotel** has the classical attributes of a slightly projecting entrance bay, and a fanlit door at the top of a flight of steps. **Palmerscross House** has a pilastered door and inscribed panel.

Dr Gray's Hospital.

RCAHMS

The Hospital was founded by Dr Alexander Gray, who had joined the Honourable East India Company and made his fortune. In 1809 he left a legacy for the founding of the hospital which included the unusual gift of $2,000 for *the comfort of virgins whose hope had decayed.*

40 **Grays Hospital,** James Gillespie Graham, 1815-19
Institutional gigantism. Gillespie Graham crammed the uses on top of each other — physicians, matron and dispensary on the ground floor, *well-lit wards, males north, females south,* on the first floor, and fever and smallpox patients on the second — so as to achieve a monumental impact at the western entrance to Elgin. He lined the top of this vast cube with a balustrade, gave it rhythm by defining each bay with a pilaster and the end pavilions by coupled pilasters, and signalled the entrance by a giant Doric-columned portico in the form of a triumphal arch. He then topped the composition with an octagonal drum tower, which mutates upwards into a circular drum with bulls-eyes, capped by a dome and cupola, all faintly reminiscent of Robert Adam's proposal for Edinburgh University. Recently converted into a modern hospital by Reiach and Hall who, during works, discovered

that the dome was being held up by little else than good fortune and spiders' webs. All is now reinforced.

West Road is fronted by a series of elegant houses and cottages, the more modern the further west. **West Lodge** has the cornice, columned porch and dressed stone of the early 19th century villa. Nos. **1-7** present a pleasing variety of porches, columned doorways and hood-moulds above the windows. The rather splendid Ingleside. **No. 9,** dates from 1815 and is thought to have been designed by Gillespie Graham: neo-Tudor

Above: *Ingleside,* West Road.
Left: 19 West Road.

glazing and details, angled chimneys and delightfully splayed corners.

41 **19 West Road** can hardly be called elegant or restrained. Built c. 1900, it is a clear product of the American virus then in Elgin. A single-storey top-lit bungalow, its porch and twin bay windows (which protrude from the corners like frogs' eyeballs) are built of huge blocks of craggy stone with carvings that seem Indian in inspiration. **Nos. 23-33** are more restrained,
42 but clearly subject to a mild infection. **Connet Hill,** designed in 1913 by Marshall Mackenzie, returns us to sobriety, although this stylish white house, with its

Above: Braelossie.
Left: Connet Hill.

ELGIN

Old Mills.

Moray Planning Dept

Below: Hamilton Drive.
Bottom: The Bield — original
drawing and as it is now.

McKean

great drum tower and oversailing roof, presages what
was to become fashionable in the 1930s. **Braelossie** is
how A. and W. Reid tackled a similar commission 50
years earlier, — a complicated Z-plan building with
spiky skyline, dormers and crowstepped gables.

The pretty, low-lying fields around the Lossie have
always attracted mills. **Old Mills** was built in the
early 19th century on a much older mill site. This
picturesque black and white mill, with its 4 ft. paddle-
wheel, pyramid ventilator and nearby granary, has
been well restored by the District Council. Open to
visitors. **Bow Bridge** was built in 1630 and bears the
legend: *Foundit 1630, Finishit 1635.* **Sheriffmill
Bridge,** an oculus above triangular cut-waters
between its two wide-span rubble arches, was built in
1803.

The **Eight Acres Hotel** is a flat-roofed example of
43 1970s geometrics. Nearby **Hamilton Drive** offers an
unusual series of flat-roofed, white houses with corner
windows and cut-away balconies in true 1930s style,
even although they were not built until after the War.

The Bield a large rubble house in Scottish Arts and
Crafts style, was designed by James Bow Dunn in
1930 to the commission of its builder Lord Provost E.
S. Harrison, whose interest in old Scots forms it
reflected.

Moray Planning Dept

RCAHMS

McKean

45 Lochindorb Castle, 13th century

Occupying almost an entire island in a bleak loch within a desolate landscape, the castle takes the form of an uneven rectangle, well built with round towers at each corner. An outer wall to the south still retains a gateway with portcullis chase. The form is native Scots, enclosing the island with curtain walls some 7 ft. thick and 20 ft. high. No trace survives of the buildings within.

Celebrated as the home of Alexander Stewart, Wolf of Badenoch, from which Highland fastness he surged out to burn Forres, Pluscarden and Elgin in 1390, Lochindorb was built by the Comyns. Edward I stayed a month in the castle in 1303 on his military progress round the north of Scotland. In 1455, James II requested the *Thane of Cawdor, my beloved squire, to raze and destroy the house and fortalice of Lochindorb, in a moorland loch beyond the Findhorn.* This he did, taking as a trophy the great iron yett which survives today at Cawdor.

46 Edinkillie

Once the hub of a large community now represented just by a lodge to Dunphail, a Church, Manse, and gigantic railway viaduct striding across a valley from nowhere to nowhere. The **Church,** 1741, is orange harled, cruciform with stone margins; windows severely rectangular, save two delightful round ones. Three small lofts survive inside. The **Manse,** 1823,

RCAHMS

McKean

Top: Lochindorb.
Middle: Reconstruction of the castle's mediaeval appearance by W. Douglas Simpson.
Above: Edinkillie Church.

Randolph's Leap got its name from a mediaeval event: the ancient family of Comyn was gradually dispossessed of its powers, and with the grant of the Earldom of Moray with Darnaway to Thomas Randolph, the Comyns of Dunphail lost their hereditary role as Foresters of Darnaway. Unwilling to cede their heritage too easily, they invested Darnaway Castle; beaten off, the Comyn of his day lived to tell only by leaping across the rocks at this spot, encouraged to this achievement by hot pursuit.

by John Paterson, in lovely orange harl with white margins, large classical windows and an oversailing roof, is not unlike Playfair's nearby Dunphail. The Churchyard has some stones of interest and an hexagonal watch house. The Bridge of Divie was built in 1831 and the railway viaduct was erected for the Grantown-Forres Highland Railway in 1861-1863 by Joseph Mitchell.

47 Relugas and Randolph's Leap

All that remains of old Relugas are the fine classical, rusticated gatepiers capped by balls. Randolph's Leap is a spectacular walk within the Logie estate down through beech and birch trees to the banks of the Findhorn and its junction with the Divie. Here can Findhorn be experienced at its most ferocious. On the banks are two markers dated 1829, indicating the flood level reached during the *Muckle Spate*. The butler at Relugas caught a salmon with his umbrella 50 ft. above normal river level.

Relugas was another seat of the Comyns. *A common small Scotch house, but an Italian front had been thrown before the building and an Italian tower had been raised above the offices, and with neatly kept grounds it was about the prettiest place ever lived in* (or so thought Elizabeth Grant of Rothiemurchus). In 1863 it was *embellished by a combination of the rarest natural and artificial beauties which render it one of the most striking and picturesque gentleman's seats in the north.* By marriage it became the home of Sir Thomas Dick Lauder who, *with all his frivolity, was a very accomplished man: his taste was excellent.* He was the chronicler of the Muckle Spate in 1829, and the Royal visit in 1843. An important vitrified fort — possibly a Pictish conical mound — survives in the grounds.

48 **Dunphail House,** 1828, William Playfair
Comyn country: and thus built for Major Charles Cumming Bruce of Dunphail. Dunphail is in

Top: Dunphail Castle.
Above: Dunphail House.

Playfair's Italianate rustic style, distinguished by asymmetry, and oversailing roof with dentilled eaves, a porch and a three-storey tower at one end. The locals thought it a *splendid modern mansion in the Venetian style*. Later alterations have eroded Playfair's original crispness.

Nearby **Dunphail Castle**, a stronghold of the Comyns besieged by Randolph, Earl of Moray, in 1330, is survived only in the vaulted ground floor and a two-storey gable with later windows, set high on the summit of an isolated rock.

RCAHMS

Logie.

The Comyns were once one of the greatest families in Scotland, Earls of Buchan, Lords of Badenoch and Strathbogie, and possessed of castles from Inverlochy in the west to Loch an Eilean, Lochindorb, Castle Roy, Ruthven, Balvenie and Rait. Members of the name included Earls of Mar and Menteith. They had the misfortune to back the wrong side in the Wars of Independence, were forfeited by Bruce and scattered. They next re-appeared, suitably adjusted, as Lords of Altyre sometime before 1492. In 1656 Robert Comyn of Altyre married Lucy Gordon of Gordonstoun, the descendants taking the name of Cuming-Gordon (or vice-versa).

49 **Logie,** after 1655

Comyn country yet: descended from the main branch at Altyre. Logie, set in a beautiful slope above the Findhorn, is a tall crowstepped, white harled house with pedimented dormer windows and angle turrets, probably rebuilt in the late 18th century, but restyled in 1860, a porte-cochère added in 1925, the north wing in the '50s by W. Ashley Bartlam. Recently remodelled by Law and Dunbar Nasmith.

50 **Darnaway,** from 15th century

Feudal heart of the powerful Province of Moray, and ancient seat of immense importance amidst one of Scotland's great forests, it is *the occasional seat of the Earl of Moray* (now, as in the 18th century). Darnaway's glory is Earl Randolph's Hall, named after Thomas Randolph, Earl of Moray, although probably built by Archibald Douglas, Earl of Moray,

One of the ladies of Logie was immortalised by Robert Burns: Bonnie Lesley, who captured Captain Robert Cumming of Logie at a London ball. Burns' poem was written lamenting her departure to London in the first place:

> O saw ye bonnie Lesley
> As she ga'd o'er the Border?
> She's gane, like Alexander
> To spread her conquests
>   further.
>
> To see her is to love her
> And love her but for ever;
> For nature made her what she
>   is
> And ne'er made sic another.

McKean

Darnaway Castle.
Above: The old castle drawn by J. C. Nattes in the 18th century. Two large towers flank the fortified gable of the Great Hall. **Right:** The unique 15th century roof. **Below right:** The castle as rebuilt from 1802.

RCAHMS

RCAHMS

in the 1450s. Unique in non-royal castles, the Hall, 90 ft. × 35 ft., retains its original collar-beam truss roof of beautifully cut timber work, with carved heads, and delicate dagger-shaped cusps — a much finer roof than, say, that of Edinburgh Castle. Little else original survives. Here, where Mary Queen of Scots dispensed justice in 1564, is preserved the famous painting of the bloodied corpse of the bonnie Earl of Moray, murdered by the Earl of Huntly in Donibristle. It bears the legend: *1591 Feb. 7: Act 24. God avenge my caus.* The castle (to which the hall was a curious appendage) was an odd, hugely picturesque collection of towers at the western end.

The new house was designed in 1802 by Alexander Laing for the 9th Earl of Moray; a large classical mansion, with castellated trimmings (possibly in homage to Gordon Castle). The windows of the central tower have Gothic glazing, all windows have hood mouldings, and the crenellated parapet is decorated with dinky turrets. Notable Georgian interiors including the entrance hall, dining room and library.

The East and West Lodges, by Maitland Wardrop, 1868, are Tudor rustic in style, with octagonal chimneys and bargeboards, and exceptionally florid, wrought-iron gates, and gatepiers capped, not with urns, but with coronets. The Victorian Darnaway Estate house style, best exemplified by the kennels and keeper's house (by A. and W. Reid, 1878), is sown throughout the vast Moray policies, with bargeboards becoming more lavish, Gothic porches and dormers, with finials on the gables.

Top: Darnaway East Gates and Lodge. **Above:** The Kennels.

51 Altyre

A barn, an estate and a quondam parish. Just so, save that the estate is that of the Gordon Cummings, the sole inheritors of the great family of Comyn. Through marriage, the family became proprietors of Gordonstoun and Dallas, which may explain why Altyre was left *a plain old building with neat modern*

Left: Altyre House (demolished). **Below:** The Italiante farm steading.

wings. In the late 19th century, Sir William Gordon Cumming was compelled to retire to his estates, and made Altyre a showpiece, with John Kinross as his architect. **Altyre House,** demolished in 1962, was 28 bays long and two-storeys tall, like a huge, attenuated stone pavilion, the entrance front distinguished only by a port-cochère and a Doric columned loggia carrying a balustraded balcony above. **Blairs House,** W. L. Carruthers, 1895, is the centre of the estate. The Italianate farm steading with its high tower and

Top: Cothall Cottages. **Above:** Altyre parsonage by W. L. Carruthers. **Right:** Dalvey House.

corbelled parapet, cottages in style nearby, may have been designed by Archibald Simpson in the mid 19th century. The stony Scots Gothic stables with crow-stepped gables, were built by Kinross in 1902, and form an attractive courtyard.

Altyre Kirk, abandoned after the amalgamation of the parish with Rafford in 1651, is a 13th century buttressed rectangle with lancet windows and Gothic doorways. **Cothall Cottages,** a handsome Cotswold-like stone terrace facing the Forres/Grantown road, were designed in 1900 by John Kinross.

Knockomie was designed by W. H. Woodroffe in 1914 as a large Arts and Crafts addition to the villa frequented by Lord Cockburn on his *Circuit Journeys* in the 1840s. Now an hotel.

Sluie

Five early 19th century salmon fishers' bothies: a lovely little terrace with Tudorish detail indicating the wealth of the salmon fishery. Visible from the countryside walk.

Knockomie is a villa — or rather a comfortable cottage with a farm — about a mile from Forres. It stands upon a sort of low knoll, and has a beautiful prospect of that little venerable old city. Except that it had no lake or stream, the place is perfect. A most excellent house in the cottage style, bright glass, a profusion of evergreens and flowering shrubs. . . . And the owner, Miss Smith, is just as perfect herself. Lord Cockburn, 1838.

52 **Dalvey,** c. 1770
Built by Sir Archibald Grant in fashionable dress: two raised storeys, entered through a Doric pilastered door, a Venetian window above penetrating into a pediment. Pilasters, balusters and urns complete the composition. Fine original drawing and dining rooms inside. Dalvey Cottage nearby is a pretty, rambling Victorian lodge with pavilion roofs and trellis round the window.

53 **Brodie Castle,** from 1567
Seat of the Brodies of Brodie since the 11th century, the 1567 Z-plan tower may incorporate parts of an earlier building. In 1645 it was *byrnt and plunderit* by

RCAHMS

Brodie Castle. **Left:** 17th century plaster vaulted ceiling.

Rodney's stone.

McKean

Lord Lewis Gordon, during the occupancy of the diarist Alexander Brodie, but much, including the exuberant early 17th century coved plaster ceiling of the Laird's room, survived. In the 18th century, the estate reached a pinnacle of development under Alexander, 18th Brodie of Brodie, who created formal gardens in the French style, with distant vistas and a canal ending in a round basin. Bankruptcy in 1774 was only staved off by the intervention of Brodie's father-in-law, the Earl of Fife. In 1787 Burns enjoyed a night at Brodie. In 1824 William Burn added a large, Elizabethan extension for the 22nd Brodie, and in 1846 James Wylson created the delightful ground-floor library out of storerooms, and added the crow-stepped form of gables, and the stencilled decor to the drawing room.

The Z-plan keep and 17th century wing are clearly identifiable, and the Dining Room (the principal chamber in the west wing) has fine but heavy late 17th century plasterwork. The entire castle was

Below: The Kinnaird tombstone in Dyke Kirkyard, drawn in 1843 by D. Alexander. **Right:** Dyke.

McKean

In Dyke Kirkyard can be found the 1613 monument of Walter Kinnaird and his wife Elizabeth Innes.

The builder of this bed of stane
Are laird and ladie of Cowbine
Quhilk twa and theirs,
Quhane braithe is gane
Pleis God, vil sleip this bed vithin.

Dyke Kirk.

Wright

renovated and reharled by Robert Hurd and Partners in 1980.

NTS property. Open to the public. Guide book available.

Rodney's Stone
Discovered in 1781 in the churchyard at Dyke, the stone forms part of a standing pillar, with excellently carved Pictish symbols. It was re-erected in tribute to Admiral Rodney: hence its name (although it is said that the name of the sexton who dug it up was Rotteny).

Wright

54 Dyke
A picturesque large village just to the east of Brodie in the centre of *fine arable fields, agreeably diversified by gentle slopes and flats, and ornamented by gardens and plantations, villas and mansions.* The Kirk, *a handsome commanding structure, neatly finished and furnished at the expense of £525* in 1781, is a noble Georgian rectangle, with round headed windows and a belfry to the west. A three-decker pulpit and original galleries survive within. The Greek revival burial place at the west end belongs to Brodie. In 1702 John Anderson founded a two-storey school for girls, but it had fallen into *irreparable decay* by the end of the century, and the 1877 school is Elizabethan with belfry and clock tower. Some well-built, later houses testify to prosperous agriculture. The nearby **Heath of Hardmuir** is ascribed by the credulous as the site of Macbeth's meeting with the witches, after which they have named a hillock. **Brodie Mill,** 19th century, a two-storey, T-plan Mill, is converted into an hotel.

55 Culbin
Now a forest offering delightful walks to the sandy shore; but under 300 years ago, the Manor of Culbin was a *populous barony,* whose long history of

occupation is proved by the find of a superb Celtic armlet. Between 1693 and 1695 the entire estate was overwhelmed beneath sand blown from the west. The Kinnaird laird petitioned Parliament in 1695 for exemption from paying dues since *the barony of Culbin and house and yards thereof is quite ruined and overspread with sand.* In 1769 Pennant recorded that *it is not long since the chimneys of the principal houses were to be seen.* In fact, you could walk among them. Not quite as speedy as Pompeii, but just as final.

The Kinnairds were ruined and sold what could be salvaged soon afterwards, including Kincorth. By 1791, half the entire parish of Dyke and Moy was under sand. Almost a hundred years later, Major Chadwick began planting trees at Binsness; in 1921 the Forestry Commission took over and the forest is now over 7,000 acres, complete with a new ecology.

56 **Moy,** John Adam, 1762

Large, plain, very unaltered three-storey house, with a pavilion roof above a cornice, erected by Sir Ludovic Grant of Grant upon the base of a 17th century predecessor. In 1762, Colen Williamson of Dyke (who subsequently went on to build the White House in Washington) rebuilt the nucleus to a design by John Adam.

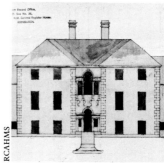

Moy House.
Above: North west elevation by Colen Williamson, 1762.
Left and top: How it was realised.

Kincorth.

The inhabitants of the country between Forres and Nairn were black as peat stacks in their appearance, the peat stack in reality generally forming part of the edifice — peat stack, peat sty and peat house being altogether. The roofs are also covered with turf or peat on which grass and heather grow comfortably. Robert Southey, 1823.

57 **Kincorth,** from 1797, altered 1869

Probably built for Robert Grant, this *handsome modern manor house* is a part of the relict of the Culbin barony sold after the ruin of the Kinnairds. A two-storey, three-bay rubble house, ennobled by ranks of Gothic Venetian windows, has been inflated with a large baronial wing, a corbelled wall-head chimney and pedimented dormer windows.

Elgin Public Libraries

Right: Invererne. **Below:** Invererne Farm Square.

RCAHMS

58 **Invererne,** 1818

General James Grant bought the estate of Tannachy on his return from Waterloo and built this fashionable seat, clearly much influenced by Dalvey House not far to the west. The principal entrance is up a flight of steps to a door with sidelights and fan-window in echo of the Venetian window above which, like Dalvey, pokes up beyond the cornice line into an urned pediment. Excellent plasterwork in the Drawing Room. The farm Square is curious: pedimented at the centre and wings, the flanks between have odd pointed windows; the tall central tower-cum-doocot like an Italian campanile.

Greshop, a traditional Scots 18th century farm harled with gabled dormer windows is somewhat over-whelmed by Forres' industrial expansion to the west. The estate fell to the Grant Peterkin family after the marriage in 1834 of Col. Grant to Mary Anne Peterkin of Grange Hall.

59 **Grange Hall,** from 1805

Similar to Invererne in the pilasters propping a pedimented entrance bay, a raised ground floor entered up a flight of steps, and a pavilion roof flanked by grand chimney stacks; but different in the extraordinary pebble rustication of the basement, the Doric porch, and the later overbearing Victorian fungus sprouting in four lacy-iron capped turrets, punctured by pedimented, round headed windows. A Greek Doric stairhall of quality survives within. It is thought that William Stark may have been the designer. A good hexagonal doocot with splayed walls, pyramid roof, and quoins, c. 1800 nearby.

THE LOSSIE VALLEY

Grange Hall.

Left: Dallas Moor drawn by Emma Black.

60 Dallas

Remote village in the beautiful upper Lossie Valley, in a plain sandwiched between the Wangie and the Hill of Melundie: a single street of mostly 19th century houses and cottages, relocated to this site in 1811. It has an overwhelming air of privacy. A single gable of Tor Castle sticks out of the plain just to the north, built c. 1400 by the Comyns (Cumings) of Altyre, and there is an older earthen motte at Tor castle to the east.

Dallas Village.

Dallas Lodge.

61**Dallas Lodge,** 1901, was added by W. L. Carruthers to the east end of the 17th century Round Square, built, similar to Gordonstoun, of rubble with crow-stepped gables. The proposed grand house of Rhininver was never built. The Lodge is a long, plain but elegant, 14 bay, two-storey building with projecting crowstep gables. The **Church,** 1793, is a harled Georgian box kirk some distance from the current village, distinguished by a belfry, a door ennobled by an architrave, a cornice and Ionic pilasters. It replaced the ancient St Michael's, *a very ancient fabric, thatched with heath and without windows save two or three narrow slits.* The unusually tall **Mercat Cross** in the kirkyard is mediaeval: a chamferred shaft with a fleur-de-lys capital. The 19th century circular complex at Cots of Rhininver is unusual.

17th century *round square* onto which Dallas Lodge was attached.

62 **Kellas Village,** in a comparably lovely setting nearby, consists of little, white, splayed-wall cottages, and the grandiose Arts and Crafts **Kellas Lodge,** 1914, on a bluff at its southern end, designed by Frank Deas in crafted stone, with towers and swept roofs.

Wright

63 **Rafford**

Tiny hamlet of scattered cottages old and new, an 1899 Free Church with wheel window and belltower and, further west, the old village by the Kirkyard: interesting items in the latter. Adjacent houses are of quality. The **Manse,** 1817, across the road, is grander Georgian with swept stairs up to a pilastered door; and the new **Kirk,** on the hillside, is a pinnacled James Gillespie Graham church, 1826, with an unconvincing tower like that at Doune (see **Stirling** volume), and pinnacled buttresses and parapet.

Wright

Top left: Rafford Kirk.
Above: The Manse from the old kirkyard.

64 **Blervie Castle,** 16th century

All that remains of a great Z-plan tower of the Dunbars is a sheer, five-storey tower punctured by later, mullioned windows. The corbelling for turrets and the wallwalk and a 1598 armonial panel survive. The first, second and fourth storeys were vaulted. **Blervie Mains,** built with stone from the castle in 1776 is a simple, two-storey house with quoins, and a projecting entrance bay. **Blervie House,** 1910, by J. M. Dick Peddie is a long, two-storey house in Scots classical style with pedimented central bay and porte-cochère. Good Edwardian interiors.

Below: Blervie Castle. **Below left:** Blervie House — original 1909 proposal by J. M. Dick Peddie.

RCAHMS

Wright

61

PLUSCARDEN

Top: Pindler's Croft, 1985, by Law and Dunbar Nasmith. **Above:** Westertown House. **Below:** The Lodge at Pluscarden. **Bottom:** The abbey crossing from the west.

OPPOSITE
Top left: Billings' drawing of the transepts c. 1846 and **top right** the Chapter House.

Westertown House, c. 1820 (demolished)
A castellated symmetrical manor in sub-Gillespie Graham manner, the entrance tower graced with a huge Gothic window illuminating the hall behind.

Pluscarden Abbey, from 13th century
Founded in 1230 by King Alexander II as a Vallisculian Priory in a secluded and extraordinarily beautiful glen. By 1454, however, it had declined to only six monks and was nearly closed for their lax and unruly behaviour. Instead, it was merged with nearby Urquhart Priory (similarly unruly), and became 65 Benedictine. Most of what survives dates from after this time.

It is probable that the nave of the church was never built, and what was, was burnt by the Wolf of Badenoch in 1390. Beautifully restored survivals include the Choir with curious side chapels, the crossing, transepts, and the east range of the cloister, containing the slype, Chapter House and Calefarium, divided into new refectory and kitchen. New single-storey buildings including a library, stores and guest rooms have been erected round the cloister site. The restoration, a considerable achievement, has been accomplished by the Benedictines of Prinknash who were gifted the Abbey by the Bute family in 1948. The North Transept has superb glass in the lancets and roundel by Sadie McLellan; and although economy has dictated a shallow-pitched roof in the recently restored choir in the place of the vaulted original, the deep red lines of the new glass create a magical atmosphere.

The quality of the Abbey is outstanding, exemplified by the composition of the great east gable of the Choir — a traceried window sitting on four lancets, capped by a large oval vesica window, and a triangular cusped window at the apex; by the carved stonework in the Chapter House, and in the carved roundel windows in the west elevation of the tower. The interior contains some of the few traces of mediaeval wall-painting to survive in Scotland. The huge window above the entrance to the slype is symptomatic of the variety and verve of odd windows throughout the complex. Other remains include the gatehouse, the Prior's lodging, and the boundary wall.

Open to the public: guide book available: shop.

Pluscarden Parish Church, 1898, Reid and Wittet
Because Pluscarden was a remote part of Elgin parish, it had no church of its own, and for much of the 19th century, the establishment worshipped in the Priory ruins. It was the Free Church that built its own: now exiled from the Abbey ruins, the new church,

Above: Pluscarden Church.

Birnie Kirk, exterior, chancel and
measured drawing.

dominated by its entrance tower, took the Abbey as
the inspiration, particularly in the decorated tracery in
the windows.

66 **Milton Duff**
Where the Upper Lossie valley flattens out to meet
the Black Burn (formerly the Lochty), Milton Duff
provides a picturesque distillery founded in 1824, and
mountains of stacked barrels. (An appropriate use for
a once notorious haunt of whisky smugglers, some 50
of them inhabiting the glen of Pluscarden at one
time.) Of the Old House, c. 1640, sold by the Brodies
to Duff, Lord Braco in 1730, only the restored, crowstepped, early 18th century doocot survives. Nearby
Pittendreigh doocot built by the Douglas family in
the 16th century, is without external pretension —
stone slabbed roof, two rat ledges, a ball finial
crowning the gable, but contains a most unusual
vaulted interior.

67 **Birnie Kirk,** 12th century
An ancient raised, walled, roughly circular Culdee site
overlooking former aerodome land (complete with Art-
Deco hangers). That it was the seat of the Bishopric
of Moray through four Bishops, who had a palace
nearby, may explain why St Brendan's Church,
although plain, is one of the best built, really ancient
churches in North-East Scotland. Its romanesque apse
is framed by a simple, round chancel-arch with
cushion capitals. The nave was later restored by A.
Marshall Mackenzie. Above the outside door into the
chancel is a much decayed cusped window.

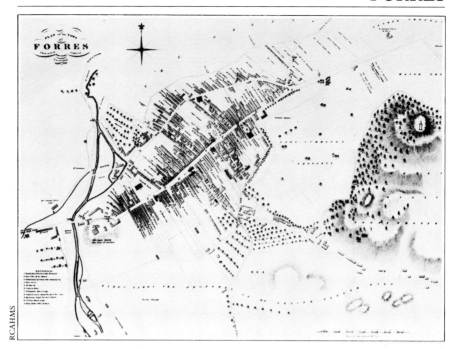

RCAHMS

68 **FORRES** *(Map p. 174)*

On the first ridge above the flood plain east of the
Findhorn River, Forres occupied a position of great
strategic importance straddling the main road from
Aberdeen to Inverness. An ancient Royal Burgh, its
original charter was renewed by James IV in 1496.
Perceived by most people as an inconvenient traffic
jam between Inverness and Elgin (until rescued by a
by-pass), it is best appreciated on a holiday or Sunday;
or by penetrating beyond the High Street, down the
wynds and alleys. Grand Victorian suburbs to the
south, and good views over Findhorn Bay to the
north.

McKean

69 **Castle**

A Royal Castle defended the west approaches to
Forres from the earliest years, washed on three sides
by the Mosset Burn. It was the probable site of the
murder of King Duffus by Governor Donald in 966,
and was insufficiently strong to prevent the burning of
the Burgh and the church by the Wolf of Badenoch in
1390. Only *poor remains* were left by the mid 18th
century, which were then used by a local Provost as
foundations for a new house which was never
completed. Now a public park, its principal ornament
is the 1855 red granite obelisk to James Thomson, a
surgeon in the Crimean War. Its eminence has been

E

Top: St Laurence.
Middle: The courtroom in the Tolbooth. The cells below were rarely used, criminals being exported to Elgin. They now house the District's archives.
Above: The Market Cross.

largely destroyed by the main road over Castle Bridge, the latest of three such, one of which was washed away in the Muckle Spate of 1829. This version is panelled, with Gothic pinnacles, designed by Peter Fulton, 1908. The Castle's defensive mound can still be perceived from Burd's Haugh.

70 **St Laurence Church,** 1904, John Robertson
A great Gothic Edwardian church, built in expensively cut, patterned stonework with plentiful spires and pinnacles, dominated by the north-eastern, deliberately designed to act as a focal point for the entire town. The transition from the simple 1775 box-kirk to this grandiose monument symbolises the third age of Forres: first the mediaeval Royal Burgh; then declining in importance to a simple country town; finally expanding with agricultural improvements and the arrival of the railway to become a major community once more in the 19th century. It is a pity that such ambition by Robertson required the destruction of the ancient Kirkyard (although the 1775 gatepiers survived). Excellent 1939 glass by Douglas Strachan within.

71 **The Tolbooth,** 1838, William Robertson
Forres' peculiar old Tolbooth had consisted of a great rectangular three-storey tower with battlements, attached to a courthouse block entered at the first floor. The tower was crowned by a later, c. 1700, three-stage cupola, the lowest decorated with imitation turrets. Robertson's replacement Tolbooth, on the same site, repeats the rectangular tower and attached block with courtroom and offices. The tower is also in three stages, but the original spire Robertson had planned was replaced by a cupola not altogether dissimilar in response to *the wishes of many gentlemen of undoubted taste who, at the same time, take a warm interest in the prosperity and ornament of the good town.* The building is transitional, caught between Robertson's undoubted classical preference (see Anderson's School), a vague Scottish revival, and growing Victorian exuberance. It has a similar sort of unreality to the contemporary tower in Dufftown, quite possibly also by Robertson.

The High Street
72 The heart of Forres faces onto *this great street,* 800 yds. long, broadening into a triangular market place in front of the Tolbooth. The 1844 **Mercat Cross,** by Thomas Mackenzie, on the site of its predecessor, is a tall, finialled and crocketted stone crown. A restoration of the cobbles around its base would be a kindness.

The High Street in 1868.
Left: The High Street looking east a hundred years ago.

Forres High Street is rare in Scotland in the quantity of pre-1914 buildings still surviving, and in the excellent preservation of its mediaeval layout, the rigs running back from the High Street even better than Elgin's. The recent restoration of 1-4 **Hepworth Lane** by the National Trust for Scotland, as part of its Little Houses Improvement Scheme has demonstrated how those characteristic houses can be brought back to life. But, save for a few cottages by the castle hill, e.g. no. **154,** dated 1668, little else pre-dates 1800. The removal of the grand 16th-17th century town of tall, harled, crowstepped houses,

Forres
A very neat town found Thomas Pennant in 1769. Dr Johnson, four years later found *nothing worthy of particular remark* save the good accommodation. Boswell was more fulsome: *an admirable Inn.* The inhabitants were always proud of it. Thus the Minister in 1793: *in point of situation and climate, it is inferior to no part of Scotland.* Five years later, the Rev. Mr Leslie thought Forres *a handsome, well built town,* with the remarkable number of 60 merchants and shopkeepers. It is from 1820 onwards, however, with improving agriculture, and particularly after the arrival of the Highland Railway, that Forres' prosperity burgeoned.

67

RCAHMS

Law and Dunbar Nasmith

Top: The 1843 Royal Bank. **Above:** The 1985 Co-op by Law and Dunbar Nasmith which replaced the Queen's Hotel. **Right:** Bank of Scotland — original drawing. **Bottom:** The bank in its setting.

McKean

It is melancholy to see a new house building even in little old Forres. Jails and schools, and such things necessary like railways and post offices, for modern accommodation must be submitted to; but a new private dwelling house introduced into Forres! with its insolent front to the street, its brass knocker and plate announcing the scoundrel's name! Cockburn, 1848.

many gable-end to the street (some with the arcades still surviving in Elgin) can be attributed to the increasing wealth of the Burgh, partly at least due to the *high state of cultivation* of the land, commented upon by Colonel Thomas Thornton in 1784. Of this earliest town, nos. **142-144** retain crowsteps at the rear. The crowstepped no. **121** carries dormer windows dated 1748, but its form implies earlier origins.

Agricultural improvements brought increasing wealth, and buildings regularly built of good stone with ranks of windows, capped by a cornice and other classical details, now faced the street. Note the pedimented windows of no. **93,** the quoins of nos. **82-86,** and the 1843 Royal Bank, no. **57,** with its rusticated ground floor, twin projecting bays, and cornice, possibly designed by William Robertson.

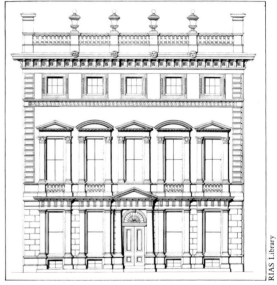

RIAS Library

73 **Bank of Scotland,** 104 High Street, 1854, Thomas Mackenzie

Built as the Caledonian Bank at a cost of £1,700 it is an excellent example of banker's Italian. Entered through a central pedimented door beneath a fanlight, the building's principal floor is marked by pilasters with curious capitals, triangular and round headed architraves, a blind balustrade at the bottom, an ornamental string course above, capped by a row of five attic windows beneath a very elaborate cornice which supports a balustrade. It is flanked by two older, pretty buildings, Dutch gable to the street.

McKean

Left: Falconer Museum.

The Falconer Museum is a memorial to a family enterprise, for in addition to the contribution of Alexander and Hugh, bequests were also received from brother Charles and three nieces. Sufficient funds, however, were never available. The museum's proposed tower and dome were both abandoned, and the architect, Alexander Reid, produced what he did by absorbing not only the building funds, but also those required to cover running costs. Within ten years, the museum's finances were in trouble, a condition that persisted until it was handed over to Moray District Council in 1975. The collection now includes, fossils, local antiquities, swords, coins, stuffed birds, and useful historical material about the district.

74 **Falconer Museum,** Tolbooth Street, 1869, Alexander Reid
Built with the bequest of Alexander and Hugh Falconer, the one a Nabob the other a scientist, originally to house a large collection of fossils (particularly from the old red sandstone) and bones. The architect was nephew of Robertson (architect of the Tolbooth) and chose what the Victorians would have called the appropriate style for a building of learning: the didactic architecture of Italian renaissance. A rectangular, two-storey building entered beneath a pedimented gable, its ground floor windows have shell-hood carving, and those of the first floor are singles, pairs, and triplets of round headed Italian windows. Note the busts of Scots botanists, engineers, etc. Cornice and urns above.

Tolbooth Street is the largest of the streets going downhill from the High Street. The buildings are pleasant, mostly early 19th century — for example no. 15 which has a pedimented centre, and pilastered doorway. The white and black **Red Lion** has a pretty dutch gable with dinky turrets, and other houses have wall-head gables. Downhill, rows of houses gable-end to the street.

Urquhart Street, although much has now been changed, consists of one and two-storey cottages, c. 1820, many gable-end to the street. **North Street** has well built cottages and houses facing the street; the cottage at no. **10** has a doorway where architrave is propped by a pair of protruberant Doric half-columns. **Tosh's Bar,** somewhat grander, is 18th century.

75 **Town Hall,** High Street, from 1823
Built by the Freemasons and extended by Archibald Simpson, 1829, when it became the Town Hall. Sold to the Mechanics Institute in 1855, it was refronted in 1901 (to keep pace with the increasing grandeur of

The Mechanics Institute.

RCAHMS

Above: Culbin Stores.
Below: High Street looking west showing the Belvedere Hotel.
Bottom: A. & D. showroom.

Top: Forres from the south in 1868. Note the train. **Far column:** The Cattle Mart and details. **Near column:** Old and new railway stations: note the cast-iron thistles.

Forres) when John Forrest applied classical columns, with polished granite shafts, topped by a balustrade. Note the flamboyant fan-windows on the ground floor. Simpson's lesser hall survives within.

93 High Street has an unusually fine classical first floor, the three windows outlined in stone, the centre one pedimented. **Culbin Stores,** nos. 132 High Street, is part of the *extensive range of substantial and elegant shops and houses with an open space in the centre* built by Robert Warden in 1808 with the proceeds of his Indian fortune, with rounded corners, classical windows, and regency fanlights. The adjacent **Belvedere Hotel** is opulent Victorian with turrets and carved strapwork. **107-111** High Street (MacKenzie and Cruickshank) is a fine classical frontage, c. 1825, with pend and distinctively craggy stonework at street level. Extraordinarily high quality plasterwork inside.

A. & D., no. 43 High Street, is Art-Deco in its pediment, the sunburst railings flanking it, and the glazing below. The entrance to the 1985 **Co-op,** designed by Law and Dunbar-Nasmith presents an asymmetrical, two-storeyed entrance capped by a roundel, re-using anthemion-leaf ironwork from the old Queen's Hotel, which it replaced. The rear facade has a louvred pediment. **St Leonard's** church, on the corner of Tulloch Park, is substantial Victorian Gothic, the gable capped by fretwork and three single cusped Gothic windows above a triple-gabled entrance. Sturdy stone spire alongside. The **Carlton Hotel,** 1900, is in florid, gabled Jacobean (an image spoilt by the dome) designed by Peter Fulton. **Castlehill Church,** 1871, presents a pinnacled Gothic gable. The neighbouring plain, 1911, stone Post-Office was thought at that time to be a *stinking monument of their cheeseparing policy.*

The **Victoria Hotel,** George Petrie, 1864, is sadly diminished by the traffic roundabout, and shorn of its former flagpole and ivy, leaving a pleasant Elizabethan building with gabled dormer windows and a pretty stone porch. The **Royal Hotel,** Tytler Street, 1867, is altogether grander: high roofs, ranks of square chimneys, and a lacy iron loggia at ground level. The **Cattle Mart,** by A. and W. Reid, 1867, was built as the Agricultural Hall symbolised by a bull's head, a ram's head and corn-sheaf which adorn the moulding around its entrance. Inside, a superb space open to the roof, galleried with a fine cast-iron balustrade, the soffit stencilled with an ochre regiment of cattle, sheep, pigs, ducks, hens, dogs and a wheat sheaf. Later king posts prop up the centre. An interesting auction-ring to one side: later walls but original steeply stepped timber seating.

79 The original **Junction Station** is survived only by a long platform canopy with fine foliated ironwork and delicate iron thistles crowning the parapet. The 1950s station is very good of its type: brick, two-storey central hall, original signs and walnut doors surviving. It is similar to 1930s Tube stations in London. A row 80 of tenements off **Market Street** has been well

McKean

McKean

McKean

McKean

McKean

McKean

McKean

Above: Royal Hotel.
Right: Restored tenements in
Market Street.

converted for the District Council by Law and
Dunbar Nasmith into smart flats with balconies,
drying greens and fashionable stair balustrades.

Some pleasant older properties survive just to the
south of Nairn Road. **Westpark,** early 19th century,
is harled with dressed stone margins. Nearby
Westpark and Louisville cottages are smaller versions
81 of the same. Oak Cottage, corner of Nairn Road and
Iowa Place is early 19th century stone. Nos. 1-6 Iowa
Place are six, original, harled cottages with dormer
windows, well restored by Moray District.

Wright

Above: Roysvale Park.
Below: Sanquhar Park.

Wright

Burd's Haugh, low-lying marshland to the south,
was developed in Victorian and Edwardian times with
substantial stone villas in ranks above Sanquhar Road,
82 overlooking Roysvale Park. **Forres Academy** is an
elegant version of the modern schools of the 1960s by
Reiach and Hall: black frame, white infill panels —
nothing superfluous. The new houses above Sanquhar
loch are a brave 1980s attempt at picturesque housing
appropriate to the hilly, wooded, watery setting.
Douce cottages line Castle Street and Burd's Haugh.

83 **St Leonard's Road,** the main road to Rafford once known as Bullet Loan, passes through the former *Hell's Hole Valley.* It is lined with some of Forres' earliest suburban houses, many immensely picturesque: Towerside, c. 1835, a classical villa with a recessed pedimented doorway; Rose Cottage (formerly Trafalgar Place), c. 1820, semi-detached, plain, red-painted houses; Craigouris, also part of Trafalgar Place, with a trellis porch; The Elms, an 18th century suburban villa with a pedimented central bay; and Cluny Bank, late 19th century, vigorous Victorian Gothic with wonderful barge boarding and angled, corner dormer windows.

84 **Cluny Hill College,** 1863, built as the Hydro, is now an education centre for the Findhorn Foundation. Against its wooded hillside, its rambling skyline of dutch gables, ordinary gables, chimneys, parapets and bays, is suitably exotic, as befitted a Hydro then, and the Findhorn Foundation now. **Leanchoil Hospital,** 1892, partly funded by Lord Strathcona, is a jewel-like 85 Jacobean toy with tower, flanked by later wings.

North Road
North Road runs along the north edge of the Forres ridge and is the second street in the town, almost entirely residential and sadly widened in places.

86 **Batchen Court,** designed 1983 by G. R. M. Kennedy and Partners turns a corner with confidence, two-storeyed, harled and slated with brightly coloured oriel windows. Most of the older houses are gable-end to the street, single storey with attic. **No. 44** has cast-

Top left: Forres Academy. **Top:** Cluny Bank. **Middle:** Villa, St Leonard's Road. **Upper:** View Bank. **Above:** The Elms.

Wright

McKean

iron railings and a wrought iron porch; the harled **no. 46** has wonderfully scrolled skewputts ending the roof slope like Mickey Mouse ears. The cottages on the corner of Tulloch Park with overhanging timber porches, are dated 1901. **The Castle,** Caroline Street, is a black and white U-plan Inn whose north wing is 18th century, maybe a relic from Shambles Wynd.

87 **Russell House** and **Sea View,** adjacent in Russell Place 1896, are decent and well proportioned: great Dutch gables, Elizabethan windows and, in Sea View, barge boards with enthusiastic fretwork decoration.

McKean

88 **Anderson's Primary School,** William Robertson, 1823

A jewel-like school founded, as is carved above the door, for the education of *the children of Forres, Rafford and Kinloss.* A simple five-bay, single-storey design, the central three-bays pedimented and advanced: the whole distinguished by a spire probably influenced by Bellie Church in Fochabers. The gigantic rear extensions are fortunately largely invisible from the front. The spire is capped by a gilded dragon.

89 **St Margaret's R.C.** is a pretty, early 20th century single-storey stone church with delicate Tudor details by John Wittet. **St John's Episcopal** was designed in 1841 by Patrick Wilson but soon afterwards remodelled by Thomas Mackenzie in a remarkably cosmopolitan manner: a great Italianate gabled and pilastered barn with a rose window facing the street, a three-arch loggia at ground level and a four-storey Tuscan campanile, the upper two stages open. **Grant Park,** opposite, was the site of Forres House, the *great lodging* of the Tulloch family and latterly the Cummings of Altyre. House and grounds were donated to the Burgh in 1924 by Sir Alexander Grant, the house being burnt down in 1971. Its site is commemorated by a sunken garden by Alistair Sinclair.

Victoria Road presents a succession of grand houses, now mostly hotels, and Forres' first real suburb. **Braeriach,** c. 1800, is a small Georgian villa

Top right: Batchen Court. **Top:** Russell House. **Above:** Anderson's primary school. **Below:** St Margaret's Church.

McKean

90 enlivened by a Doric columned porch; **Cluny** is a smart regency house, with a flat pavilion roof, entered through a recessed, pedimented doric portico. The **Ramnee Hotel** is opulent Arts and Crafts complete
91 with half-timbering and a round tower. **Park Hotel** is in rich merchant's Scottish, crowstepped gables, animal finials, gargoyles and fine plaster work, hall and staircase within.

92 **Drumduan**
The original early Victorian, single-storey villa, raised ground floor and projecting gabled eaves, once set in beautiful grounds and orchards, was extended in the late 19th century and upwards (to its severe detriment) in 1912. Now restored by the Findhorn Community.

The Lodge is contemporary, in like style. The **Witches Stone** is set just south of the Main Road beside Bronte Place (during whose construction the stone was broken and used in the building before being retrieved). Of uncertain origin, it is said to mark the spot where the tar barrel containing a convicted witch came to rest after it had been rolled down Cluny Hill prior to immolation.

93 **Sueno's Stone,** possibly 9th century
23 ft. high cross slab carved with a wheel cross on one side and carvings of a battle on the other, including a number of headless corpses. This side is divided into separate panels: nine horseman, above ranks of armed soldiers, above headless corpses and skulls, above foot-soldiers and horsemen, above more headless corpses. The name Sueno's Stone derives from Boece's supposition that it recorded Sueno's victory over Malcolm II in 1008, but the style is earlier, and may instead commemorate a victory of the Picts over the Danes.

94 **Nelson's Tower,** 1806, Charles Stewart
Octagonal, Gothic, harled tower, with corbelled crenellated parapet topped by a flagpole. One of

Top: St John's Church. **Main:** Cluny. **Upper:** Park Hotel. **Above:** Forres House by G. R. M. Kennedy.

Stewart's first public monuments to the memory of Nelson, it was built both as a viewpoint and the centre piece of the landscaping on Cluny Hill. Splendid views from the summit.

KINLOSS

Very flat — which explains the R.A.F. station (the main employer for much of this part of Moray); very fertile — which explains the location of one of Scotland's finest abbeys; and very beautiful.

95 **Kinloss Abbey,** from 12th century

Little remains of this, one of the great religious houses of Scotland, founded by King David I as a Cistercian abbey in 1150. Old engravings confirm 18th century descriptions of *specimens of the most beautiful Gothic architecture.* Two rib-vaulted chambers, one converted into a chapel, part of the cloister wall, and ruins of the abbot's lodging, now survive. They are all clustered together amidst splendid table tombs and other sepulchral monuments, on a gentle mound on the edge of the river Erne (now Kinloss Burn), overlooking the Laich of Moray.

Above: Sueno's Stone sketched in the mid 18th century. It was certainly much less eroded 200 years ago, but some allowance for fantasy must be made. **Top right:** Nelson's Tower. **Right:** Kinloss Abbey in the 18th century.

Kinloss Abbey

Why such grandeur has been reduced to a rickle of stones in a peaceful graveyard mound, is explained by the predator — Alexander Brodie of Lethen. He observed that *the buildings were far more extensive than were requisite for a Kirk, and the stones were excellently squared, large, and well calculated for buildings of strength.* Brodie agreed to provide a new place of worship for the parish *with which they were well pleased,* and then had *full liberty to pull the abbey to pieces; with barbarous haste he did so, making traffic of the stones, many of which were bought for building the Castle in Inverness,* in 1651.

Not that Brodie was the only person so minded. Its own Abbots were likewise: in 1470, Abbot James Guthry sold the organ, a silver basin, and an ewer, and had to be prevented from resetting the painting above the altar. Some Abbots were driven to such extremes by shortage of money; not so Kinloss, one of the richest endowed houses in Scotland, whose powerful Abbots were mitred. According to Ferrerius, who was in Scotland in 1520, Kinloss had 150 feather beds, 28 arras coverings, two silk beds and pewter vessels. The library was very well stocked and the church ornamented with paintings, statues, organs and altars.

The Kirk, 1765, is unusually elegant: a T-shaped, harled rectangle with great square, hoodmoulded, stone-mullioned windows, a mock-Gothic 1830 crenellated tower at the eastern end. The fact that the 1820 **Manse,** a harled classical building with a pedimented entrance bay, was designed by James Gillespie Graham could indicate that the church tower was his also: it has his stamp. A pleasant row of stone cottages nearby.

Top: Kinloss Abbey a hundred years ago. Note the Queen Victoria look-alike. **Middle:** The site today. **Left:** Kinloss Village and Church.

FINDHORN

RCAHMS

Kinloss Abbey.
Above: Ruins of the Abbot's house. **Below:** Processional doorway to the cloister in the south wall.

RCAHMS

The **R.A.F. estate** is mostly remarkable for being very English in design and layout, and private. There are good buildings of the English 1950s vintage, and some recent additions in red brick. Kinloss House is a rather splendid Victorian baronial turretted extravaganza.

The bell in the Kirk was made in 1688 by John Cui or Cowie, mort-bellmaker of Elgin:

> The dead I be waile
> The quick I allarm
> That nought ther is
> Can death's force charm

Sea Park, early 19th century
A plain house reclothed in Elizabethan fashion, c. 1830, with mullioned windows, crenellations and 96 ranks of tall, octagonal chimneys stacks, hugely embellished with further extensions, battlements, a conservatory and planned gardens in 1842.

FINDHORN

Wright

97 The third village of the name, its predecessors standing to the north west in the mouth of the bay. Sometimes, at dusk, you have the sensation that they, and Culbin Manor just across the water, are still there. Modern Findhorn post-dates 1701, when its predecessor, *regularly built upon a pleasant plain* was overwhelmed in a single tide: a tide which also created much of the current Burghead Bay. An 1843

Findhorn from the north.

OPPOSITE
The Crown and Anchor at the heart of Findhorn. **Below:**
Findhorn from the south-east.

Gazetteer recorded: *fears are entertained that the village itself must again be deserted. A piece of land here called Binsness has already been destroyed.* What the elements failed to destroy, modern sprawl, pavements and tourism came close to achieving. Matters are now improving.

The village straggles along the north-east crescent of Findhorn Bay, and consists of rows of fishermen's cottages, laid gable end to the water in the normal manner, *stryplies* being the name for the lanes between them. The heart of Findhorn is the square around the

McKean

Crown and Anchor, 1739, a white crowstepped inn of great charm. **Kimberley Inn** is similar, but with a forestair, and dates from 1777. **Quay Cottage** is a slightly grander house with a moulded and corniced doorway, a datestone on the front inscribed *James Rose Margaret Simpson 1773.* **The Yacht Club** (Findhorn House) is an amalgamation of an 18th century house with 1890 enlargements. The **Main Street** is faced with some grander two-storeyed houses, one elevated by painted quoins and margins

McKean

The Moray Floods or *Muckle Spate.*

On 3rd August 1829 observers from Sutherland noted with just foreboding an enormous black cloud which had settled over the Monadhliath mountains. It emptied some 10 ins. of rain onto parched ground, swelling the Spey, Findhorn, and Lossie to levels never since experienced. At Relugas, where debris washed down by the **Findhorn** was blocked by the narrows, the river level reached 50 ins. above normal. It surged out to engulf the entire flat lands around Forres, destroying both Findhorn and Forres' bridges. Ships from the port of Findhorn were used in the rescue operation, the following being extracted from the log of the **Nancy:** *Sailed at half past ten a.m. Tide High. In danger of foundering from trees and other land wreck. Set all sail, scudded with a fair wind over Mr Davidson's farm — steered for a small house on the estate of Tannachy — Rory Fraser, his daughter and two laddies, terribly fleggit, were landed aboard — bore up and steered a S.W. course — passed over dykes and cornfields — made for Waterford — current nearly swamped. Found John, his wife and two other women. Got them on board, safe, but sair druckit.*

The **Spey** destroyed all the bridges at Knockando, came near to destroying Telford's new one at Craigellachie, flooded Rothes, took out most of the new Spey Bridge at Fochabers (together with one of the crowd who had trusted the sturdy new structure), wrecked nine ships at Garmouth and seemed, at one time, about to immolate Kingston entirely. Even the gentle **Lossie** joined the fun. The main street of Dallas became a canal, Kellas was submerged under 20 ft. of flood, Bishopmill bridge was washed away, for a short time Elgin seemed isolated upon an island, and the great loch of Spynie made a dramatic, if brief, re-appearance. The final toll of the flood was the destruction of 22 bridges, and 60 houses. 600 familes were made homeless and six people killed.

Wright

It is difficult to realise, now, just how important a port Findhorn was, or how great was the loss when the arrival of the railway rendered it redundant. It was the principal port of Moray. In 1798 it had four large boats trading with London, three trading with Leith, two with Aberdeen, and four of its own fishing boats. In addition, it freighted up to 100 further boats in fish bait. Imports included sugar, tea, silk, cotton, and hardware from London; leather, tallow, soap, iron, farm utensils, glass and furniture from Leith; coal from Sunderland and ropes and flax from Aberdeen. The principal exports were grain and salmon. Its method of curing and drying haddocks gave the fish the name of Findern Speldings.

Findhorn Foundation
The Findhorn Foundation was started in 1962 by Eileen and Peter Caddy, and Dorothy Maclean, in the unlikely location of the caravan park beside the port of that name. It has now blossomed into an extensive teaching and publishing charitable operation, able to offer residential and other courses. In addition to its new Universal Hall, the Foundation owns the former Hydro at Cluny Hill, Drumduan, and Newbold Houe, (all in Forres) and the delightful Isle of Erraid, by Iona. The purposes of the Foundation are difficult to summarise easily. Its activities are based on an attitude to humanity, to the notion of community, to whole earth and to spiritual experience which cuts across contemporary behaviour patterns. The members of the Foundation believe their approach offers the chance of a rich and fulfilling life, involving art, movement, music, dance, craftwork, gardening and self analysis. On the one hand, a clear child of the '60s; but on the other hand, a vigorous survivor, demonstrating that the ideals of the period had more substance than is currently credited them.

Findhorn

round the window. On the **Salmon Greenie** may be found both an ice-house and a pill-box. The **Kirk,** 1843, is stone, with a pretty tower, lunette windows and the original gallery within.

The **Universal Hall,** Findhorn Park, was designed in 1974 by George Ripley as an Arts and Conference Centre for the Findhorn Foundation, who also use it for Community Meetings. It reflects the Foundation's own mystic beliefs in its plan and use of glass, stained glass by James Hubbel, and timber.

98 **Milton Brodie,** 1835-41, probably by William Robertson
A delightful courtyard house, snug in a sheltered glade surrounded by trees, belying its original name of Windy Hills. Robertson re-orientated and transformed the entire building by adding an unusually beautiful, feminine south front, flanked by two-storey,

Top: Laich of Moray looking south over Gordonstoun. **Right:** Elgin Cathedral from Cooper Park. **Above:** Elgin Cathedral — west processional doorway.

pedimented gables capped with twin chimneys, and decorated with anthemion leaves. Note particularly the scrolls. A four-column Ionic porch leads into the single-storey central wing and hallway. The earlier house thus refaced, on the ancient site of the house of the Chantor of Moray, consists of a standard two-storey house, c. 1700, with later wings. There is an octagonal 18th century garden house with pyramid roof, and a 1661 sundial (purchased from Harrods!).

99 Crook of Alves

A small agricultural community identified from the Forres-Elgin road by a pleasant 1895 Gothic school and contemporary stone houses and cottages. The old village lay to the north, by Kirkton. The **Old Kirk,** built 1769-71, now lies abandoned in its ancient churchyard; a plain, harled oblong with belfry, with a series of different sized round headed windows. The **Parish Church,** a mile and a half south west, built as a Free Church in 1878, is quite imposingly symmetrical, with pilastered sides, and a three stage bell tower, capped by urns and a balustrade at the centre.

Top: Milton Brodie, a neo-classical gable detail below. **Above:** Alves Kirk. **Right:** Alves Old Kirk.

100 Burgie Tower, late 16th century
Erected for Alexander Dunbar, Dean of Moray, some
time after 1566, Burgie is a sheer six-storey tower,
relic of a large Z-plan building. It stands complete to
its crenellated, corbelled wall head. Each room is
15 ft. square, the bottom vaulted as usual. The arms
of Dunbar, dated 1602, sit over the great fireplace on
the first floor. **Burgie House,** a 1912 rebuilding of
the 1802 house built with the stones of the castle, is a
plain, two-storey granite house with a columned
porch. **Burgie Lodge,** c. 1840, is an aberrant three-
bay, two-storeyed house transformed by the projection
of square bay windows flanking a two-storey, recessed,
entrance bay formed with pilasters.

Top left: Burgie Castle in the 18th
century. **Above:** As drawn by
Billings in 1846 and is now.
Below: Newton House in its new
neo-Billings dressing. **Bottom:**
The Oakwood Motel.

Sweethillock Farmhouse, 18th century, is
traditional with skewputts and a gabled porch.
Rheeves Farmhouse is older, harled and crowstepped. The scant remains of **Asliesk Castle** recall a
substantial 17th century house of the Brodies: L-plan,
the long hall on the first floor, a corbelled stair tower
leading upwards, and the usual turrets.

101 Newton House, 1852, carefully disguises its 1793
classical origins behind the spiky baronialism of its
symmetrically placed turrets, and crowstep-gabled,
orielled entrance bay. The Laird had clearly popped
out to buy the newly published *Billings' Antiquities*
and got a few new ideas. **Duke of York Tower,**
1827, crowning the atmospheric Knock of Alves, is
octagonal Gothic with a crenellated parapet, standing
within a substantial prehistoric fort, parts of whose
ramparts are still identifiable. The 1821 **Toll Cottage**
has a Doric columned door and Tudor chimney
stacks.

102 Oakwood Motel, 1932, Dougal and Andrew Duncan
Erected in the days when the car was a pleasure, and
driving out for Sunday tea a treat, the Oakwood is a
road house of split and unsplit logs and timber
shingles: a rustic imagery appropriate for its wooded
setting, although its style is indoubtedly influenced by
Dougal's stay in Canada.

McKean

McKean

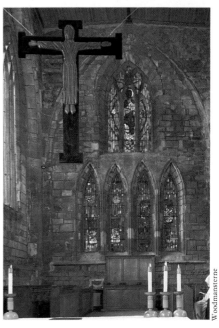

Woodmansterne

Top: The River Findhorn at Relugas. **Top right:** Brodie Castle. **Above:** Pluscarden Abbey. **Right:** The interior of the restored Choir.

Moray District Libraries

Left: Forres a hundred years ago from Breakback. **Below:** Duffus Castle, the ancient Loch of Spynie converted to corn. **Bottom:** Roseisle and the Burghead promontory from Findhorn.

McKean

McKean

85

BURGHEAD

McKean

RCAHMS

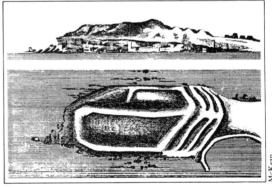

McKean

Top: Burghead Harbour. **Above:** Aerial view showing the grid-iron town dug into the headland. **Right:** As drawn by Mazell in the 18th century.

BURGHEAD

103 Almost certainly an island or long promontory in the Dark Ages, Burghead was a major centre of Pictland, protruding into the Moray Firth. Even now, its 80 ft. high tip is crowned with the damaged remains of an outstanding Pictish fortification which 18th century engravings show as medallion-shaped; a ridge running along the centre, and protected on the landward face by three, 800 ft. ramparts in arrowhead formation. These walls were timber-laced and nailed at the joints. The fort was mutilated after the construction of the port, from 1805, and of these fortifications only the central ridge survives. **The Well,** thought to be early Christian in date, consists of a 11 ft. rock hewn chamber reached down stone steps. It was discovered in 1809.

Above: Disused warehouse by the harbour. **Left:** The height of the headland above the sea is clearly apparent.

By 1843, Burghead was largely as we see it now, the houses *substantially built with freestone and slated.* The echoing **Harbour,** 1807-10 (extended 1881), is lined with early 19th century three-storey stone granaries, one reconditioned as a Boat Centre in the 60s, with an upper balcony, weatherboarding and flagpoles. One now unroofed, lies awaiting beneficial re-use: five bays long with small square windows like a galleon. An 18th century Kirkyard with some picturesque slabs and table tombs lies up toward **Doorie Hill,** which is the sole survivor of the cross rampart. The houses are varied, two-storeys, some with pediments above the door, or datestones, frequent dormer windows and the occasional barge board. **The Museum,** 16-18 Grant Street, has displays of local history, archeology and fishing. Grant Street also contains the two churches: the **Free Church,** 1851, presents a bellcoted gable to the street. Opposite, the **Parish Kirk,** c. 1890s, is

Burghead was one of *the most celebrated places of rendezvous of the buccaneers from Norway. The vast ramparts still remaining bear the weightiest testimony to its great strength. . . . The triple ditch and rampart are yet neat and entire. The top had been defended by logs of oak piled on one another. Many pieces are still to be seen half-burnt.* Charles Cordiner, 1780.

In 1805 a group of landowners bought an old fishing village from Sir Archibald Dunbar to lay out a regular town of straight parallel streets, a port at the top. In 1818, William Young of Inverugie became sole owner and developed Burghead into Moray's principal herring fishing station and a major exporting port of grain, thus contributing to the decline of Findhorn.

Burning of the Clavie takes place annually on the 11th January at the 19th century Doorie Pillar on the old fort. A half tar-barrel is fixed to a stout 5 ft. long pole by a hand-wrought nail hammered in by a stone. It is lit by a peat then marched blazing round the burgh before being cascaded down the slope. A suitably pagan ritual for this strange place.

The Well in 1843.

Garmouth.

McKean

Coulard Hill from Old
Lossiemouth painted by
Emma Black.

(Cllr Mrs Shaw) White House photography

Kingston at the mouth
of the Spey.

McKean

McKean

McKean

The River Spey
Top: The view upstream to Boat
of Brig from Ordiequish. **Above:**
Birds prey over the estuary at
Tugnet.

opulent Gothic, a stone broach spire to one side and a fine porch. The adjacent school with its spired bellcote and grouped gables was built in 1886.

Cummingston, founded 1808 by Sir William Gordon-Cumming, became the home of the masons of nearby quarries: a single street of plain stone cottages facing the main road.

104 HOPEMAN

Founded as a fishing port in 1805 by William Young of Inverugie, and expanded with the new harbour provided by Admiral Duff in 1838 for exporting stone from the quarries. **The Church,** 1854, is cruciform with a Tudor Gothic tower donated in 1923 by an Elgin distiller. The town takes the form of a grid-iron following the road downhill to the harbour. An **Ice House** for the storage of fish, mid 19th century, has an unusually well built entrance, like that of an Egyptian vault. **Hopeman Lodge,** c. 1840, a harled Italianate seaside pavilion with dressed stone margins and a pedimented porch, was built for Young of Inverugie.

Top: Burghead Kirk and School.
Above left and right: Hopeman.
Below: Hopeman Lodge and shore from the harbour.

Inverugie House, Alexander Reid, 1864
A grand single-storey home built of dressed stone, with a pavilion roof, a Corinthian columned porch and iron verandah.

105 NEW DUFFUS

Moved to this site from the neighbourhood of the old
Kirk in 1811, the village consists of two parallel
streets of pleasant, harled cottages running along the
hill. Slightly grander houses incorporating classical
details, line the bottom road to the old Kirk. The
Well House, 1815, has classical proportions. **The
Church,** A. and W. Reid, 1869, is a Gothic box with
a curiously attenuated spire, almost detached
alongside. The **Manse,** 1830, is appropriately grand
for this wealthy spot; a two-storeyed, coursed rubble
house, wings projecting, pavilion roofs, regular
windows, and pilastered doorway.

Duffus House, early 18th century
A handsome modern seat placed in a small park, it was
built for Archibald Dunbar of Thunderton, and
consists of a long, three-storeyed, harled block,
extended in 1840 with servant's quarters, crowsteps,
another wing, and a corner tower. A two-storey hall
inside.

106 Duffus Old Kirk, St Peter's, from 1226

Once at the centre of Old Duffus, but now secluded in
the bosky surrounding of table tombs, St Peter's is a
spacious, dignified, roofless chamber with rectangular
windows, and an outside stair. There survives, of the
earlier church, a fine Gothic porch erected in 1524 by
the rector Alexander Sutherland, the mediaeval vaulted
ground floor of a tower against the west end
containing some carved stones, and a balustraded
burial enclosure on a mediaeval base. There are some
exceptional sepulchral monuments and a Kirkyard
cross. Note particularly the beautifully carved 1616
Keith tablet in the east gable, the neo-classical Dunbar
burial enclosure with a pedimented centre with
anthemion leafs like Milton Brodie, and the curious
monument to Abraham Leslie.

Top: New Duffus cottages.
Upper: View along the old road to
the church. **Above:** Duffus House.

107 Duffus Castle, from 1151

Rising like a battleship above what used to be Spynie
Loch, the castle consists of a large outer bailey
circumferenced by a wet ditch, a walled and ditched
inner-bailey, and a great stone keep on top of a motte:
a survival unique in Scotland. The motte-and-bailey
plan, a Norman manifestation, dates from King David
I's import of Norman nobles to Scotland, and, in
particular, the translation of Hugo Freskyn from
Strabock (West Lothian) to Moray, whence he drew
his title *de Moravia*. In the late 13th century the castle
was held by Sir Reginald Le Chen for Edward I, and
it was burnt by Scots patriots in 1297. The keep
probably dates from the rebuilding. The Castle was
sacked again in 1452, after which new buildings —
including a hall — were built against the north

Memorial stone in the kirk.

McKean

The fishing coast. Above and **Right:** Buckie. **Bottom right:** Portknockie skyline from Cullen. **Below:** Findochty.

McKean

McKean

McKean

McKean

Cullen
Above: The square, Mercat Cross
and original route to the old town
and the castle. **Below:** Cullen
House from the Punchbowl.

McKean

McKean

Above: Duffus Kirk in its bosky setting. There are some magnificent tombs.
Right: Aerial view of Duffus Castle showing a clearly defined moat, outer bailey and stone keep sliding down the *motte*.
Below: The castle rising out of the Laich as it would have from Spynie Loch.

RCAHMS

McKean

curtain. It was finally abandoned in the late 17th century for Duffus House.

The three-floor Keep is the most striking survival, particularly since the north corner has sheared off and slipped part away down the motte. Well built, lancet windows lighting the staircase, rooms and passages in the wall thickness, the keep contained a great hall on the first floor.

Nearby **Mid Mains steading** has been cleverly converted into a house and office by Ray Marshall.

Duffus Castle Keep.

108 GORDONSTOUN

Of all the gentlemen's seats in the broad province of Moray there is not one surrounded with such traditions of popular superstition as that of Gordonstoun. (Lintie of Moray).

The Gordon family acquired two bogs in the 15th and 16th centuries: the Bog of Plewlands and the Bog of Gight. Growing grandeur required some retitling: and they became Gordonstoun and Gordon Castle respectively. Plewlands began life as a tall thin rectangular tower, maybe 16th century, with single-storey wings. In 1616 the 1st Marquis of Huntly added two elephantine, two-storey wings, with gnome-like corner turrets dwarfed by a heavy pavilion roof. In 1730 (the date of the north doorway) the tower was domesticated, and in 1775 given the classical facade we see today. The northern is the best: flush with the wings, faced with well-cut ashlar stone, and graced with a centrally placed, pedimented, coupled Corinthian-columned door. The wings were clearly refaced and quoined contemporaneously, the rear of the turrets sliced through to accommodate. By contrast, the garden front — although regular and balustraded, is thoroughly rubbly: the wings project beyond the facade which shows clear traces of bits and pieces of old masonry: something the vaults on the ground floor confirm. The flat roof behind the pediment was clearly intended as a promenade, to judge by the cap-house giving access to it. Although much of interest survives within, it is really a working school interior, but the staircase, and the great Drawing rooms on the first floor are of particular note. Axially placed facing the south front is the graceful Canal, centrepiece of the garden layout, and putting the proclivities of the Bog of Plewlands to enlightened use.

In 1934 the house and estate were taken over by Dr Kurt Hahn for Gordonstoun School, whose attitude to education was to encourage self-reliance and independence. Of the new buildings, note: **Cumming House,** designed as a timber *open square* by George Kennedy in 1939, using timber naval construction — a hull-shaped pediment above the main door; and **St Christopher Chapel,** 1966, designed in the jagged profile, ribbed-concrete, convex walled style of the time by Patrick Hughes.

Upper: Cumming House.
Above: The Chapel.

Top: Ben Rinnes from the Moor of Ballintomb. **Above:** Tomintoul. **Right:** The temple of Pomona at Cullen.

McKean

McKean

McKean

McKean

McKean

RCAHMS

Above: South facade of Gordonstoun. Rubbly protrusions from the castle are still visible.
Left: The polished, classical, north front.

The beehive doocot, 16th century, on a mound beside Gordonstoun House, is one of four. Sir Robert, so it was said, misliking his spouse, believed the adage that the construction of a doocot brought a death in the family, and tried four times! Unfortunately, they are of different ages, one converted from windmill to doocot in 1731.

The justly celebrated **Round Square** was built in the late 17th century, and now harbours study rooms, classrooms and the library. It is predominantly two-storey, the taller sections, marked by crowstepped gables, having an attic storey in the roof.

Below: The celebrated *Round Square.*

RCAHMS

The Michael Kirk.
Right: Interior looking west.
Top: Detail of the west window with its flower-carved spandrels.
Above: The chapel in its setting.

109 **Michael Kirk,** 1705

A grey, remote, deserted looking edifice thought Robert Billings in 1846. Built as a mortuary chapel over the remains of the Wizard on the site of the ancient Kirk of Ogstoun, the Kirk is now reached along a hushed, enchanted avenue from Gordonstoun. One of the pillars guarding the entrance to the raised, tree-bound enclosure is graced with a rude, vigorous carving of a bearded savage, seemingly in a loincloth, standing on an upturned leaf, a club over each shoulder, a crude Ionic capital acting as halo. His twin can be seen top right in the 1705 Gordon memorial inside the chapel, one cudgel less. In 1900 the Chapel was roofed, furnished and fitted as an Episcopal Chapel by John Kinross for Lady Gordon-Cumming. It was reconditioned for use by the school before the construction of St Nicholas, the altar oddly at the west end.

Architecturally, it is pure 15th century Gothic, two hundred years late, beautifully built without the slightest hint of historicism or revival. The window tracery is remarkable, enhanced by flower-carvings in the cusps. The Gordon Monument, surging from floor to ceiling, is overblown rustic baroque. In the graveyard survives mediaeval Ogstoun Market Cross topped by a five-pointed cross, and some fine tombstones.

The Wizard

Sir Robert Gordon, 3rd Baronet of Gordonstoun, succeeded his father Sir Ludovic in 1688. Educated abroad, and a keen amateur chemist (a correspondent of Boyle) he soon earned the reputation of being a wizard, the circular form of the steading being attributed to necromantic requirements. There must have been somewhat more to his behaviour than that to earn the fantastic legends which surround him, although the ancient atmosphere of the Bog of Plewlands and the palpable mystery of the Michael Kirk, may have encouraged the credulous. In 1839 William Hay immortalised Sir Robert in endless verse, recording a legendary death very similar to that of Don Giovanni or Doctor Faustus. At the appointed hour Sir Robert, who had already forfeited his shadow to the Devil in Paris, was snatched by his new owner as he rode desperately for sanctuary at Birnie.

Sir Robert could drink like a
    Morayshire chiel —
But a man has sma' chance that
    would drink wi' the Deil;
Sir Robert got faddled; — when
    upstarted his guest
On all fours — an' nicker'd in
    shape o' a beast.
Gee up! Cried Sir Robert, an'
    sprang on the back
O' that fierce-looking charger, so
    fiery an' black;
An' bang through the window, for
    Birnie are boun'
The Devil and Sir Robert o'
    Gordonstoun!
Losh! sic a queer loon
Was this Morayshire loon!

His son, also Sir Robert, is not reputed to have been a warlock: only *dour, litigious, irascible, despotic and ill-conditioned.*

The mysterious guardian to the Michael Kirk. A heraldic savage, certainly, but *just* heraldic?

Covesea Lighthouse.

The Caves, cliffs, and beaches are celebrated. The Laird of Gordonstoun hid his horses in one to prevent their being commandeered in the '45. The Sculptor's Cave has produced bracelets of German origin, c. 700 BC. It also has Pictish symbols such as crescents, V-rods and fish incised into the roof. The most westerly, Helg's Hole was customarily inhabited by tinkers. *Some of them are lofty even from the entrance,* recorded the **Muckle Isaac** in 1798. *Others, with a low entrance, become gloomily lofty and uncomfortably damp within. Others are low, dismal, dark and damp. Another behind the village of Lossiemouth had, in ancient times, been formed into a small hermitage: it was completed by a handsome Gothic door and window. . . . These artificial decorations were torn down (c. 1768) by a rude shipmaster.*

View to Lossiemouth.

110**Covesea**
The Skerries lighthouse, designed by Allan Stevenson in 1844, is a tall, white elegant pencil with a corbelled parapet, set off by a flat-roofed keeper's house with grouped square chimneys and projecting pedimented bays.

111**Kinneddar**
The site of a *strong fortress* of the Bishops of Moray, thought to have been a large courtyard castle on a hexagonal plan the ruins of which were still visible in the early 19th century. The old Kirkyard lies just to the south, inside which still stands the column of the Mercat Cross. Fragments of Pictish stones confirm Kinneddar as a Pictish site of the first importance. The stones are now in Elgin Museum. Here also paused the Cathedral of Moray in its progress from Birnie to Spynie prior to settling at Elgin. **Drainie Old Manse,** a pleasant, classical house with bracketed eaves, c. 1845, by A. and W. Reid, with an enclosed, pilastered porch, is now the Captain's House for Gordonstoun.

The 18th century **Coulard Bank** farmhouse, reflects the fertility of the district: a grand, black and white cube, raised above a basement, with a pavilion roof. A comparable house in many other parts of the country would belong to the Laird.

R.A.F. Lossiemouth was founded in 1938, and is out of bounds. The control buildings — chunky geometric blocks with horizontal windows — seem in period. Just after the Second War, the aerodrome expanded causing the demolition of Gillespie Graham's Drainie Old Kirk, whose 1821 panelling is in Gordonstoun House, and some stonework in St Christopher's.

McKean

LOSSIEMOUTH

Old Lossiemouth was laid out by the burghers of Elgin in 1764 on flat land on the left bank of the Lossie. Its character has been eroded by the expansion of Branderburgh, by the damage inflicted by the arrival of the now vanished railway, and by post-war neglect. The **Mercat Cross**, 1700, a circular shaft on a five-step base, is at the junction of the old and new towns: the **Seatown,** on the far side of Spynie Canal was part of the 1764 feu, and displays the characteristics of squat cottages built low, in rows, gable-end to the sea. Most of the houses are c. 1830s. The new town to the west, is grid-iron in plan, exemplified in the well-built stone houses of **Gregory Place;** in no. 1 Ramsay MacDonald was born in 1866. **Clifton Road** has rather grander houses: nos. 19-21 are 18th century with a forestair; the tall **Lossiemouth House,** no. 33 with its circular stair tower was built c. 1750. **Rock House,** 1789, is much grander, with quoins, lacy ironwork lining the steps, and skewputts. There are some interesting new houses by G. R. M. Kennedy and Partners, and a dominant new High School to the west.

The popularity of Lossiemouth, we are told, *originated with its golf course.* 1,000 years earlier, St Gerardine enjoyed life in a 12 ft. square cave overlooking the sea. *The Port of Lossy, otherwise of Spynie,* first appears in 1383 when Bishop Alexander Bur appealed to the King to resolve a dispute with the burgesses of Elgin who were trespassing on *his water of Lossy.* The original port was adjacent to Spynie Palace, and was only moved to its current location in 1698 after the mouth of Spynie Loch had become closed with shingle. Lossiemouth is now really three communities: the old (and largely forgotten) fishing village post-1764; Branderburgh, laid out on the cliff-top to the north to a design by George MacWilliam, c. 1830, named after the landowner Col. Brander of Pitgaveny; and Stotfield, an old fishing village facing due north whose one-storey thatched tenements commanded *a high rent as summer quarters* as long ago as 1868.

McKean

Top: Branderburgh from old Lossiemouth.
Left: St Gerardine's.

LOSSIEMOUTH

Coulard Bank Hill is lined by villas and churches dominating the plain below from Prospect Terrace. **St Gerardine's,** 1901, is a clever design by Sir John Burnet: white-harled, red roofed, a squat tower with twin romanesque windows, a composition greatly improved by a long low block extending to the west. The interior is plain but elegant. **St James's,** 1888, by A. Marshall Mackenzie, has a stone spire beside a now mutilated Gothic window, although the fine doorway below survives. **Prospect Terrace** is lined with pleasant stone bungalows and grander villas including Craigmount, c. 1870, Tower House, and Viewmount with its Italianate belvedere.

Branderburgh was developed as the new town of Lossiemouth became saturated and the harbour by the Seatown unable to cope with the volume of new boats. George MacWilliam's plan was focussed on St James' Square and a grid of streets running northwards downhill to the sea. Contemporary with the move, the Burghers of Elgin caused the foundation of a new **Harbour** at Stotfield Point in 1837, designed by James Bremner of Wick. It became a centre for a new herring fishing fleet, and it was here that the first of the new Zulu class of fishing boats was built in 1879. **Pitgaveny Street** runs along the side of the new harbour, where there can be found the **Fishery and Community Museum,** converted from the grand old warehouses by Wittets. It contains scale models of fishing boats, the old Covesea light mechanism and a reconstruction of Ramsay MacDonald's study. There has been little change to the street since it was first built: good, two-storey stone buildings, warehouses toward the northern end where the Museum is located. **Steamboat Hotel,** corner of Queen Street, plain and regular in black and white, has a marvellous example of the cut-away corner.

113 The openness of **James Square** dwarfs the small stone houses, church and shops which enclose it. However, the former **Regal** cinema by Alec Cattanach

Top: Old Market Cross. **Middle:** Gregory Place, birthplace of Ramsay MacDonald. **Above:** Fisheries and Community Museum. **Right:** The Harbour.

102

Ramsay MacDonald (1866-1937) Britain's first Labour Prime Minister was born at Lossiemouth in poor circumstances in 1866. He entered Parliament in 1906 representing Leicester, and was elected Leader of the Party in 1911. Losing his seat just after the war, he returned in 1922 representing Aberavon and in 1924 became Prime Minister in the minority Labour Government. In 1929 he became Prime Minister for the second time. In 1931, at the depth of the recession, he formed a National Government which many Labour members regarded as a betrayal. He retired in 1935, and was buried two years later in Old Spynie kirkyard.

Top left: The plain steep streets of Branderburgh. **Left:** Steamboat Hotel. **Below:** The Town Hall. **Bottom left:** Edwardian Stotfield and golf. **Bottom:** *Blucairn.*

(now a furniture store), was smart of its type with its horizontal windows, black, green and yellow tiles, and three huge storm prow fins soaring up over the roof. Brilliant repainting could repay the effort. The **Town Hall,** High Street, by Reid and Wittet, is tall and curiously truncated: generally Italianate with tower to match. Some interesting houses uphill to the south with Tudor chimneys and mouldings. The 1862 **Baptist Chapel** in King Street, is a good essay in Gothic revival. **Stotfield** is Edwardian plush — large hotels and guest houses, with bays, gables, projecting lounges and ironwork, uncertainly hovering between rediscovered Scottishness and imperfectly recollected Elizabethan. Some fine houses along the ridge to the west — notably F. W. Troup's **Blucairn,** 1906, Arts and Crafts in its tall, tiled gables. The town is now looking rather battened down. It needs to face and overcome the challenge presented by the lure of warmer, cheaper climes. The beaches are still splendid.

Top: Spynie Palace and loch as they survive today. The palace is under a programme of restoration and consolidation. **Above left:** Mazell's view of the palace in the 18th century. **Above:** Billings' view c. 1846. Note the superb entrance gateway on the right.

Left: View in 1805 showing remnants of the old lochside village. **Below:** Old Spynie Kirkyard.

114 **Spynie Palace,** late 14th century onwards
One of the most splendid mediaeval monuments in
Scotland. In 1200 Bishop Richard moved the
Cathedral of Moray to Spynie, where it paused for 24
years, and his successors fortified the strong headland
poking into Spynie loch for their own use. They
remained there long after the Cathedral moved on to
Elgin. Over the next two centuries, they built the
grandest surviving Bishop's Palace in Scotland, awe-
inspiring even today, with the loch mostly drained by
Thomas Telford (1808-12) and the Palace in ruins.
Soon to be revealed by repair, consolidation,
excavation and interpretation.

The ruins consist of a late 14th century castle of
enclosure, strengthened by great towers at each corner.
The gateway, with its cutwater projections and
corbels, bears the arms of Bishop John Innes
(c. 1406). There are clear remains of an ancient indoor
tennis court, and a chapel; but the ensemble is over-
shadowed by Davy's Tower: that built by Bishop
David Stewart, 1461-1475 in response to a threat by
the Earl of Huntly to *pull him from his pigeon-hole.*
One of the largest tower-houses in Scotland, it is 60 ft.
high and 60 ft. long, with four principal storeys above
a vaulted ground floor, and five bed chambers in the
wall's thickness. Several armorial panels.

115   **Old Spynie Kirk,** although a stone's throw uphill,
has to be reached by a wearisome road detour. Of the
Kirk itself little survives, a great Gothic gable
collapsing in the early 19th century. That gable was
the last surviving relic of the pre-Elgin Cathedral, the
east end of which is marked by a beautiful mediaeval
wheel cross head on a 19th century base. The tree-girt
graveyard gazes down on the Palace and loch beyond,
and is graced with good graves, including Ramsay
MacDonald's.

116   **New Spynie Kirk,** was built to the west in 1736
following a shift of population, and its raised hillside
site commands a good view over the Laich. All that
distinguishes it from a well-built cottage is the
steepness of the roof, and the pointed doorway and
Gothic bellcote both thriftily resetted from the old
Kirk. The 17th century cut stone on the smaller door
has been re-used upside down. Coombed plaster
ceiling, traditional layout and loft inside. The Manse,
now **Quarrywood House,** was designed by A. and
W. Reid in 1844, and its nearby 16th century **Doocot**
is now converted to a water cistern.

117 **Findrassie,** 1780
The seat of the Leslies of Findrassie is a tall, austerely
elegant, Laird's house with steeply pitched roof,
quoins and fanlight. Large, harled, vaulted outbuildings, and a 1631 crowstepped doocot.

Top: Cross marking eastern end of
former cathedral.
Middle: Graveslab in Spynie
Kirkyard.
Above: New Spynie Kirk
overlooking the Laich.

Pitgaveny House.

Above: Pitgaveny Stables.
Below: Inchroom. A 1756 Innes house whose name recalls the former island nature of this place.

118**Pitgaveny,** 1776
Built for James Brander, a successful Lisbon merchant, this great house once commanded a fine prospect over the Laich but is now snuggled by trees. It is a huge classical cube, pedimented on the principal, west front (its columned entrance now obscured by a substantial, enclosed porch), grandly extended to the east. The principal rooms on the first floor retain original features. A conical 18th century Doocot and a dramatically crowstepped farm steading.

Innes, 1640-1653
In 1157 Berowald from Flanders received a charter from Malcolm IV for the lands, almost an island, between the Lochs of Cott and Spynie. It is probably 119 from the word *Inch* or *Innis* that Berowald's descendants took their name.

Built for the Innes of that ilk, this tall, elegant building exemplifies the transition from tower to house. (Barely a few miles away, in 1644, another Innes saw fit to opt for the tower, rather than a house, in Coxton). William Aytoun, *Maister Maissoun at Heriott* was paid £26:13:4d. for providing a plan on paper for Innes which, when the account was finished in 1653, had cost £15,266 Scots.

The plan is a simple development of the L-plan tower house, with the staircase in the heel. The principal rooms are still on the first floor. Aytoun's skill lies in how he identifies each feature, and then creates a total design therefrom. Each window has its own carved tympanum (some round, some like pediments) standing out from the harling and the skewputts are wonderfully carved with animals or crocketted finials. Each floor is outlined by a string course. The verticality of the composition is completed by dormer windows, groups of elegant,

Innes.

square chimneys set on an angle, and by the staircase tower, taken a storey above main parapet level, balustraded and flat-roofed for a promenade. Aytoun thereby demonstrated the extent to which the Scottish castellated tower house was in reality an excellent house-form once stripped of its defensive features.

Home of the Tennant family during this century, the interior contains excellent original panelling. The Walled Garden with its many rare trees, part by Sir Robert Lorimer (1916), is open to the public, and contains a 17th century sundial, a summerhouse on timber legs, and Lorimer gatepiers. The 1830 Coach House and Stables designed by William Robertson were much altered by Walker and Duncan in 1916. Marshall Mackenzie's 1872 North Lodge is big and baronial with oriel windows. The early 19th century East Lodge is picturesque Tudor; but the West Entrance, the principal entrance up the avenue of trees, is dignified by octagonal gatepiers and screen walls.

Leuchars.

120 **Leuchars,** early 19th century

A pleasant 19th century villa, a projecting, gabled eastern wing with triple round-headed windows above a drawing-room bay. The chimneys are grouped, villa-style, and there is a lacy timber regency pergola. The house is part old: there is a 1583 datestone and an early 17th century sundial. The Innes of Leuchars built a *handsome house* in the mid 18th century, drained the land and raised plantations of oak, ash, witch elm, larix and Scotch fir. The current fertile state of the land is attributable to their efforts.

Above: Sheriffston, drawn by Emma Black. **Below:** Longhill Mill. **Bottom:** Elm Cottage, Urquhart.

[121] **Sheriffston,** c. 1850, A. and W. Reid
Very mid-Victorian recast of an earlier house in a handsome revival of Scottish renaissance: harled with dressed stone margins, grouped octagonal chimneys, finials, string course, pedimented dormer windows, and projecting stone bay windows to the principal rooms.

RIAS Library

St Andrews Llanbryde Parish Church, 1796, a long stone box with round-headed windows and bellcote, is
[122] rather more dignified than the normal Georgian God-box.

[123] **Longhill Mill,** 1733 (rebuilt 1891)
Two-storey T-plan mill, the kiln identifiable by its slated octagonal vent. The overshot wooden wheel and internal machinery survive intact. The mill merits preservation as one of the finest survivors in the north east.

[124] **Urquhart**
A priory was founded by King David I in 1125 in this most fertile and equable spot, and granted extensive lands and rights including Fochabers and the Spey fishing. However, in 1460, the Valliscaulian monks at Pluscarden *becoming licentious* and expelled, the Urquhart Benedictines (whose reputation was even worse) moved, bell, book and candle south west, abandoning their patrimony. By the late 18th century the ruins could be discovered only *with difficulty* in a hollow north east of the old church, in the lands of Wester Clockeasy farm. A carved wheel cross built into the Church hall wall is the only relic.

RCAHMS

An old Burial Ground with 18th century tombs recalls the old church. The current **Parish Church** on Gas Hill, 1843, was designed by Alexander Reid (in the style of Gillespie Graham), on a location north of the village selected by the Earl of Fife who, at that time, had not only Innes but the entire parish save Leuchars. Unusually orientated north/south, the church is entered through an English crenellated tower symmetrically set in the gable. The parapets and Gothic tracery of the windows are delicate Perpendicular in style. A 1751 skull and cross bones monument brought from the earlier church commemorates a Minister, Robert Tod.

McKean

The **Manse,** 1822 is appropriately classical, with a pilastered door, fanlight and cornice. The nearby doocot is contemporary, unique amongst doocots in its construction of clay dab. The tiny **village** is not as pretty as it was. Thatch is replaced by slate, the verges and flowers by pavements and garden walls and the formerly ivy-clad Free Kirk gable, closing the

vista, is stripped and mutilated by a garage door. **Elm Cottage** is Tudor, like a tiny Sheriffston, gables and square chimneys.

125 **Llanbryde**
Picturesque, almost English, village, cruelly bisected by the Elgin-Aberdeen road, and remorselessly extended to the north. A tree-girt, table-tombstoned, abandoned hump identifies the site of the *extremely ruinous and insufficient* kirk demolished in 1796. The Innes of Coxton enclosure is harled; there is a 1612 graveslab and a group of buildings between the base of the hill and Longhill Burn retains traces of the delightful picturesqueness of the village before the expansion of the main road. Most dominant is Thomas Mackenzie's Scots-Elizabethan style **Tennant Arms Hotel,** 1854, contemporary with the remodelling of the entire village into a long curving street of cottages with front gardens and trees. Houses to the east are more recent, and include a fine stone shell porch (1859) and a good '50s police station. The Crooked Wood to the north offers walks and orienteering courses.

McKean

Top: Urquhart Village photographed by Ian Lindsay 50 years ago. **Above:** Urquhart Church.

Left: Llanbryde, drawn by Emma Black, showing how pretty it could look were it not for the road.

Right: Coxton Tower drawn by Billings c. 1846. The ladder was replaced by stone steps within months of this engraving being made.

McKean

Although it has been said that Sir Alexander Innes chose his form of house as a result of his attachment to the old ways of doing things, the almost unique nature of Coxton implies a stranger motivation — the fear of fire: resulting, perhaps, from the universal horror at the suspicious burning of Frendraught Castle in 1630.

RCAHMS

Speymouth Manse, 1732, a substantial, white two-storey building with scrolled skewputts, had the distinction of quartering the officers of first the Jacobite, and then the Hanoverian officers as the armies marched west to Culloden in 1746. The Hanoverians got to drink the *fine home-brewed beer* which the Minister had prepared for the Jacobites.

126 **Coxton Tower,** pre 1644

Four-storey fortified tower built for Sir Alexander Innes, cadet of Innermarkie, and grossly anachronistic for that date. Predators were discouraged by its two corbelled turrets. The first floor entrance was reached originally by ladder (the stairs added c. 1846 by Benjamin Pennycuick), and was additionally defended by the projecting bartizan above. Innes feared fire as much as foe, for the walls are thick, each floor stone vaulted, and the roof stone-slabbed. A fine armorial tablet above the door.

Nearby **Pittensair** Farm, is dated 1735 on a skewputt, its west gable inscribed James Ogilvie and Margaret Stewart. Harled with dressed stone margins, the house has thick stone chimneys, a semi-circular stair tower, and panelled doors. Ogilvie was the local master mason responsible with the Minister for the new Parish Church at Speymouth, and his house at Pittensair is a miniature version of the fashionable house of the time: not unlike the way that master mason Bauchop's own house in Alloa was a scaled down version of those he had built for grander patrons (see **Clackmannan** volume).

127 Speymouth Church, 1733

In 1731 Speymouth Parish was amalgamated from Dipple, Essil and Garmouth, and this simple, belfried harled church opened in 1733. Inside, a 1634 pew back from old Dipple Church *Ericit be Valter Hay and L. Innes his spouse.*

128 Garmouth

In 1587, much to the anger of the Elgin burghers, the Innes' port (originally Garmach) was erected into a Burgh of Barony with a Cross, harbour and annual fair on 19th June. It grew rapidly to considerable trade, but now that the Spey has shifted, its port is difficult to visualise.

Now high and dry, and extremely pretty, Garmouth's disorderly, picturesque streets form a pleasing contrast to the regularities of Fochabers, Lossiemouth, Cullen, etc. It is particularly notable for the clay-bool (sea-washed stones bonded with clay and sand) construction of many of its old houses. The **Muckle Isaac** in 1798 explained how they were built: *The walls of the greater number of the houses in this village are composed entirely of clay, made into mortar with straw. . . . In building this kind of wall, it is necessary to suspend the work a little, on the addition of every yard in height, that it may not warp from the perpendicular. . . . It is frequently raised to two-stories, wears a slated roof, and is neatly finished within. If sufficiently covered on the top, it is found as durable and more impervious to wind and damp, and appears as handsome, when daubed over on the outside with lime mortars, as walls of stone in the common fashion.*

The principal street is **Church Street,** which winds its way from the prominent, 1845, somewhat proturberantly bellcoted Free Church, down to The High Street. Its neighbour, the 18th century Garmouth Hotel has a corniced door. **The Neuk,** later 18th century, is harled with stone margins —

Top: Speymouth Kirk. **Above:** Stynie farmhouse.

In June 1650 Charles II landed at Garmouth, from Holland, on his way to be crowned at Scone, in defiance of Oliver Cromwell. The Scottish Commissioners who had treated with him in Holland had done so on the condition that he would subscribe to the Solemn League and Covenant, and his decision to land in the north may have been influenced by the fact that one of the Commissioners was Brodie of Brodie. There was no regular landing place at that time, and legend has it that the future King landed piggy-back on the shoulders of the Garmouth ferryman, Milne. Almost immediately ashore, he was pressed to honour his pledge by subscribing to the Covenant: in short, a somewhat brusque welcome home by his subjects.

Left: Garmouth, looking down to the Spey.

Garmouth was a major port, with the export of timber floated down the Spey from Rothiemurchus, export of salmon and grain, and the import of coal and iron goods. In 1792, over two large ships a week sailed from Garmach with cargoes of timber or salmon. In 1804, it had two sawmills and 36 ships' carpenters.

Top: Garmouth Church.
Middle: Dellahapple House.
Above: The schoolhouse.

plain Scots classical. **Dellahapple House,** an early 19th century cottage villa, is dignified by a Doric portico reached up a flight of steps. **Eastfield,** Spey Street, is dated 1734 and initialled AA, and beautifully yellow harled with cut-stone margins. The door is dignified by a pediment. There are several other buildings of considerable architectural interest, not least the curious **School House,** an asymmetrical, almost Art-Nouveau building on the hill, constructed of concrete. Several houses in **The Brae** are rendered clay. In a now vanished house, King Charles II was persuaded to sign the Solemn League and Covenant on his arrival from Holland in 1650.

129 **Kingston**

In 1784 Messrs Dodsworth and Osborne of Kingston-upon-Hull contracted with the Duke of Gordon for all the timber from the Forest of Glenmore. They constructed a dockyard named Kingston, (after Hull), and constructed boats of up to 500 tons, with masts over 60 ft. high.

The balance of Kingston's occupation was the export of Highland timber from the Rothiemurchus forest. *The logs and spars belonging to the English company are at times floated down in single pieces, to the number of perhaps 20,000 at a time, conducted by 50 or 80 men going along the sides of the river to push them off by poles as they stick on the banks, hired at 1/2d. per day and a competent allowance of spirituous liquor.* The woods began to be exhausted c. 1860, at which time the changing course of the river and increasing size of ships spelt the end of almost 100 years prosperity for Kingston and Garmouth.

It is an odd place, crouching low against the sea like a whaling station. Two streets of heavy shouldered white cottages shelter beneath the bank of shingle. Virtually all houses were washed away in the Muckle Spate in 1829, save **Dunfermline House,** a large, early 18th century house with perhaps earlier origins, used variously for salmon storage, and lodgings for the shipyards; long and rather elegant with architraved doorways. **Seaview** has skewputts carved with lion's heads.

130 **Mosstodloch**

Distinguished by the giant Baxter's of Speyside factory. Founded in the Victorian period in a shop in Spey Street, Fochabers, the first factory opened here in 1916. The Old Shop was rebuilt here, joined in 1986 by a new Visitor's Centre designed by the Ashley Bartlam partnership. Audio visual and tours round the factory, to watch canning of items as various as Royal Game soup to Cullen Skink.

McKean

131 **Toll House,** Spey Bridge, c. 1830
Possibly designed by Archibald Simpson, who was
involved with repairing the bridge after the Muckle
Spate, it is delectably built in great blocks of polished
stone, a bracketed architrave above the door and
windows, and wide-eaved roof carrying ornamental
iron brackets. Not quite a twin brother to the East
Lodge to Gordon Castle.

Spey Bridge, opened 1804
Until this bridge was built, the Spey, with its
notorious and dangerous flash floods, could only be
crossed by the ferry of Boat of Bog. Built by George
Burn, perhaps to a design by Thomas Telford, in
1801-04, the bridge was an elegant three-arch bridge,
an oculus above each cutwater. The Muckle Spate
washed away the two western arches, which were
replaced by a single timber arch, designed by
Archibald Simpson, in turn replaced in 1852 by a
cast-iron version, a wooden model of which is in the
excellent Fochabers folk museum.

In 1809, Elizabeth Grant of
Rothiemurchus visited the
Rothiemurchus timber-yard at
Garmouth: *On leaving Duffus we
drove on to Garmouth to see Mr
Steenson, my father's wood agent
there; he had charge of all the timber
floated down the Spey from the forest
of Rothiemurchus where it had grown
for ages, to the shore near Fochabers
where it was sorted and stacked for
sale. There was a good-natured wife
who made me a present of a milk-jug
in the form of a cow, which did duty
at our nursery feasts for a wonderful
while, considering it was made of
crockery ware; and rather a pretty
daughter, just come from the
finishing school at Elgin, and stiff
and shy of course. These ladies
interested me much less than did the
timber-yard, where all my old friends
the logs, the spars, and the deals and
my mother's oars were piled in such
quantities as appeared to me endless.
The great width of the Spey, the
bridge of Fochabers, and the peep of
the towers of Gordon Castle from
amongst the cluster of trees that
concealed the rest of the building, all
return to me now as a picture of
beauty. The Duke lived very
disreputably in this solitude, for he
was very little noticed, and, I believe,
preferred seclusion.*

Ashley Bartlam

Elgin Library

RCAHMS

Top: The Spey at Mosstodloch. **Above:** The
Spey Bridge at Fochabers. The original two bays
are on the right: that on the left replaces the part
washed away in the *Muckle Spate*. **Above right:**
Baxter's reception centre. **Right:** The old Toll
House before extension.

McKean

Old Castle Gordon drawn in 1672 by Captain John Slezer.

132**Gordon Castle and Fochabers**

The dinner hour was 7.00 p.m. precisely. The number at the dinner table of Gordon Castle was seldom less than 30, but the company was continually varied by departures and arrivals.

We passed through files of servants to the dining room. It was a large and very lofty hall, supported at the ends by marble columns, within which was stationed a band of musicians, playing delightfully. The walls were lined with full length family pictures, from old knights in armour to the modern dukes in the kilt of the Gordon plaid; and on the sideboards stood services of gold plate, the most gorgeously massive and the most beautiful in workmanship I had ever seen. The band ceased playing when the ladies left the table; the gentlemen closed up and the conversation a merrier cast, coffee and liqueurs were brought in when the wines began to be circulated more slowly; and at 11.00 p.m. there was a general move to the drawing room. Cards, tea and music filled the time until 12.00, and then the ladies took their departure, and the gentlemen sat down to supper. I got to bed somewhere about 2.00 a.m.

Nathaniel Willis, 1834.

The lands of the Thane of Fothopyr were cruelly washed by the Spey. For centuries, they were known simply as the Bog or, latterly, Bog of Gight (Windy Bog), remembered in Boghead and Bogmoor. Old Fochabers was on the highest ground in the marsh, and **Roman Camp Gate** indicates the probable site of one of the string of Roman land camps between Stonehaven and Bellie.

In the 14th century, the forest of Enzie had been given to Sir John Gordon by King David II. George Gordon 2nd Earl of Huntly, began old Castle Gordon after 1479, and his grandson (also George) greatly extended it into the magnificent, moated Renaissance palace drawn by John Slezer in 1672, and described thus by Richard Franck in 1656: *Boggieth the Marquis of Huntly's palace all built of stone facing the ocean, whose fair front worthily deserves an Englishman's applause for her lofty and majestic towers and turrets that storm the air and seemingly make dents in the very clouds. It struck me with admiration to gaze at so gaudy and regular a frontispiece, more especially to consider it in the neuk of a nation.*

Probably Z-plan, old Castle Gordon was dominated by the huge, flat roofed, six-storeyed tower, part of which still protrudes from the earth like a dead tree. The linking block was reminiscent of Amboise, unusually favoured with an open loggia at first floor level and well endowed with decorated dormer windows; a further tower on the far side. There were outbuildings and statues, like Cawdor. Had it survived, it would have far outshone Craigievar in its Renaissance exuberance.

Duke of Buccleuch

RCAHMS

Above: John Baxter's 1769 proposal for the south facade.
Left: As built.

It was the age of enlightenment. In 1769 Alexander, 4th Duke of Gordon and 18th *Gudeman o' the Bog,* invited the architect John Baxter to rebuild the Castle, insisting that part of the original tower was incorporated. The result, a long, castellated building 538 ft. long, was called variantly *the most magnificent edifice north of the Forth* and *the pride of Scotland.*

The Ducal palace of Gordon had all the problems of gigantism and few of the benefits. Its saving grace was the six-storey central survivor, as the symmetrical centrepiece to the tall, battlemented central pavilion; otherwise it was a tedious quarter mile of two-storeyed crenellated regularity. The landscape, the interior painterwork and furnishings, and the lifestyle — best recalled by the American journalist Nathaniel Willis in 1824 — were truly sumptuous.

Boghead (the Home Farm) pleasantly symmetrical, harled with round-headed windows, was probably designed by Archibald Simpson in 1829. **Lakeside House,** late 18th century, is an odd, flat-roofed, slate-

The Dukes of Gordon dying out, the estate was inherited by the 5th Duke of Richmond and Lennox in 1836. Gordon Castle became a secondary seat and was eventually sold to the Government in lieu of death duties in 1938. The present owners, Gordon-Lennox descendants, bought the Castle in 1953 by which time its condition had deteriorated following army occupation. Social circumstances no longer provided the necessary army of servants. The central block was razed to the ground save for the six-storey tower, the east wing, by John Baxter and Abraham Roumieux was restored and adapted by Schomberg Scott as a substantial, quadrangular, castellated mansion, the west wing used for farm and offices.

Below and left: Gordon Castle now.

RCAHMS

Elgin Library

Burns visited Castle Gordon in 1787 and paid his dues in what we might now call poet-laureate bread and butterese:

Wildly here, without control
Nature reigns, and rules the
    whole;
In that sober pensive mood
Dearest to the feeling soul
She plants the forest, pours the
    flood.

Life's poor day I'll missing rave
And find at night a sheltering
    cave
Where waters flow and wild
    woods wave
By bonnie Castle Gordon.

The old village of Fochabers had clustered around old Castle Gordon. Although a burgh of Barony, it had declined to the *wretched town* visited by Pennant in 1771, many of whose houses were ruinous when Johnson and Boswell passed through two years later. It offended the Duke's improving principles and detracted from the splendour of his new palace. It had to go. Of the old village of Fochabers there survives a thatched cottage, used until recently as the castle fruit store, *tastefully fitted up and surrounded by a verandah.* Nearby is Fochabers' old 12 ft. high cylindrical **Mercat Cross,** of uncertain date.

Gordon mausoleum, Bellie Kirkyard.

hung, corniced house with a Venetian window, and panelled, circular rooms on ground and first floors. The **East Lodge,** early 19th century, is much in the style of Archibald Simpson, derived from Playfair: octagonal oversailing pyramid roof, horizontally proportioned glazing, bracketed cornices, and a pedimented projecting entrance. The **Main Gate** is crenellated, and flanked by crenellated classical lodges, of a kind with the Castle. The large Doric column in front is the 1920 War Memorial.

133 **Bellie Kirkyard,** site of the old kirk prior to the move to Fochabers, shows little trace of it. Its glory is the statuesque mausoleum to Duchess Jean, c. 1825, an open temple of 12 Ionic columns. Some of the table tombs have carved classical palmettes on the uprights.

134 **FOCHABERS**

Fochabers, John Baxter, from 1776
Like most planned towns of Moray, the new Fochabers straddles a main road — the great road from London to Inverness via Aberdeen. Laid out as an east-west parallelogram on raised ground, flanked to the south by the Burn of Fochabers, and to the west, by the Spey, its heart is **The Square,** dominated by the Church, originally facing down the axis to the Episcopal Church: the vista spoiled (as in Fife Keith) by the grossly insensitive siting of the bus shelter and lavatories.

Most of the homogeneous **High Street** is early 19th century. No. 79, built as the Union Bank sports a pilastered doorway and architraves. The c. 1800 **Gordon Arms** is one of the *several good inns* noted in 1843, black and white with engaged Doric columns, cornice and architrave above the door, and a courtyard behind.

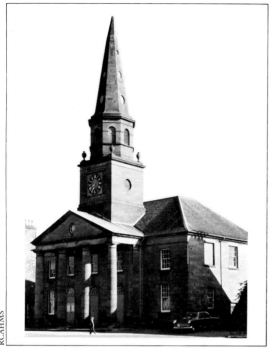

RCAHMS

RCAHMS

Bellie Church, John Baxter, 1798
The only building of national standing in Fochabers, lending as touch of a most European sophistication to this otherwise plain town. Comparable to Baxter's now demolished other church in Callander (see **Stirling and the Trossachs**), its regular windows, clock tower and pedimented Georgian portico are as redolent of the establishment at rest as are town halls. The planning has been cranked to squeeze the requirements of a Church into a classical box of considerable presence. Galleries inside.

It is flanked by two fine, two-storey houses, c. 1800, whose blind, semi-circular arcades lend the Square a sophistication the town finds otherwise elusive: one

Left: Bellie Parish Church, Fochabers. **Above:** Episcopal Chapel. **Below:** The High Street.

The Inn here is excellent wrote Lord Cockburn in 1842. *And if the village had been less regular, and less obviously withdrawn in its structure from the will of people, it would have been better. But the truth is that during the lives of the last two Dukes it was neither meant nor used as a village for villagers, but as a kennel for the retired lacqueys and ladies — maids of the castle, and for the natural children and pensioned mistresses of the noble family, with a due proportion of factors, game-keepers and other adherents of such establishments as their two Graces and their households rejoiced in.*

I wasted an hour on Gordon Castle, which I despised so much when I first saw it above 40 years ago. I find it as contemptible as ever. Cockburn, 1839.

McKean

117

Right: South Street. **Above:** St Mary's. **Below:** The Folk Museum. **Below right:** Milne's High School. **Bottom:** Gordon Castle East Lodge.

the Manse, the other former estate office. Opposite, closing the Duke Street vista, is the Gordon **Episcopal Chapel,** an early Gothic revival, finialled box sprouting amidst trees, designed by Archibald Simpson in 1834; church upstairs, the windows glowing with pre-Raphaelite glass; Episcopalian school, now the Rectory, downstairs.

South Street, open to the south, is one of the nicest thoroughfares. No. **46** has a pedimented doorway, and No. **42,** 1845, some crisp *Greek-Key* ornament lacing the porch. **St Mary's** is pretty: finials, crenellations, three delicately Gothic traceried windows, all in a smooth ashlar finish. The vista of **East Street** is delicately closed by the Castle's East Lodge. On its east side some interesting stone-and-dormered terraces. On the corner, the **Fochabers Folk Museum** carved from the 1900 Pringle Church. The stained glass and lovely timber barrel-vaulted roof, are easy to appreciate from the upper gallery of coaches and bathchairs.

Milne's High School, Thomas Mackenzie, 1846 A pretty, symmetrical, Scots Elizabethan building, all crockets and finials, crenellations, cloisters and turrets. Skyline is all. This big courtyard school was founded by Alexander Milne (1742-1839) who was driven to emigrate and make his fortune in New Orleans because his master, the Duke of Gordon, had objected to the length of his hair.

Off West Street, on the south side of the Burn are a number of large, interesting buildings, particularly **Speybank.** The **Winding Walks,** reached from opposite White Gates on the Buckie Road are delightful, leading uphill to an excellent viewpoint called The Peeps.

Off the main road to Buckie, by the Boghead entrance to the Gordon estate, is a red painted, two-storeyed timber **Chalet** with balcony, c. 1820, allegedly designed by the Duke himself who had visited Geneva. There is speculation as to the purpose for which he intended it.

Spey Bay consists of a straggle of exposed, sea-whipped houses, an unusual driftwood summerhouse, the rump of a rebuilt hotel, an enormous windswept shingle ridge, a reedy estuary, a remarkable metal-trussed railway bridge (1886) now pedestrian, and Tugnet.

135 **Tugnet Ice House,** 1830

Three gigantic, cavernous brick-vaulted chambers, only the very top of which protrude above their protective earth and shingle plinth commemorate the

Left: Tugnet Ice House. **Top:** Swiss villa. **Above:** Driftwood summerhouse, Tugnet.

Below: View from Tugnet over the Spey estuary to Kingston.

TYNET

We soon entered the country called the Enzie, where very different maxims prevail from those that have improv'd the Cullen estate — This Country is inhabited entirely by Papists, whom the family of Gordon retain here, thinking they pay higher rents than any one else would and who, obstinately adhering to their antient agriculture, are little able to pay the smallest rent. Carlyle, 1765.

Top: Tynet Chapel interior.
Above: Leitcheston doocot, the only survivor of an old Gordon manor hereabouts.

once principal salmon fishing station on the Spey, employing over 150 people. The fish were stored in the ice house pending export, the ice collected from the river and lochs, and pushed into the caves through openings high in the wall.

Beautifully restored by the District Council with an interesting exhibition. Open to the public.

The adjacent **Square,** its elegant two-storey front block, circular entrance and wall-head gable, 1783, housed the Manager, a store, and the boiling machinery.

The Enzie
The forest of Enzie was the first Gordon property in Moray, and it became famous for the Gordons' religious persuasion: Roman Catholicism. The 1st Duke established a Catholic Chapel at St Ninians in 1687, the Episcopalians being driven off to Glasterim for their own services. The current **Kirk,** 1887, is a simple bellcoted box with florid Gothic windows. Nearby **Leitcheston Doocot,** 17th century, is a steep, stone slated, crowstepped, doocot, its four little doo dormers leading into four little, separate doo dormitories.

136 **St Ninian's Roman Catholic Chapel, Tynet,** 1755
Symbolic of the survival of Roman Catholicism in Banffshire, St Ninian's is probably the oldest building purpose-built for Catholic worship after the Reformation still in use. Since it was erected when Catholicism was proscribed, the exterior was intended to be indistinguishable from a white-harled fermtoun or row of cottages; indeed it was adapted from a *small little house where a poor woman had lived for some time.* The interior, beautifully restored by Ian Lindsay in 1951, however, is a transformation. A timber Corinthian columned inner doorway, leads into a long, white, coved-ceiling chapel.

PORTGORDON
Founded in 1797 by the 4th Duke of Gordon,
137 Portgordon was for a long time the largest port on this section of the Moray Firth. By 1874 its harbour was able to accommodate 350 ships, and it had an extensive export of corn. It is now wholly empty. The mostly Victorian village is laid out on the flat shore, a square surrounding the plain, well-built Victorian church, a Gothic bellcote above the gable. The houses are mostly two-storey stone, with painted door and window surrounds, some with the added distinction of hood-moulding above window and doors, quoins, string courses and, in Gordon Square, distinctly curious dormer windows.

Portgordon.

138 BUCKIE

At shore level, a three mile straggle of older fishing ports — Nether Buckie, Easter Buckie, Yardie, Ianstown, Gordonsburgh and Portessie, split by the Burn of Buckie which runs into the sea by the old Seatown. In the early 19th century, a new town was laid out along the ridge behind which shares, with the other planned towns, the common characteristic of a long street, (East and West Church Streets) focussed upon a square (Cluny Square) with this difference, that no main road passes along it. The Victorian town

Left: Buckie from the west.
Below: The North Parish Church.

is big, rubbly, windswept, lacking enclosure and somewhat harsh and impersonal: plentiful unsubtle crowstep gables, dormer windows, pediments and turrets — all the details money could buy. Its monuments include **North Parish Church,** 1880, by Duncan MacMillan on the site of William Robertson's 1835 chapel, which symbolises Buckie's Victorian

McKean

Buckie Harbour.

In 1877, John Gordon of Cluny put up £60,000 for the construction of **Cluny Harbour,** which provided Buckie with one of the finest harbours in Scotland and explains the explosion of late Victorian prosperity along the cliff top. **The harbour** is always fascinating, with its slipway, drawbridge and Fish Market (best on Thursdays and Fridays). The Maritime Museum, Cluny Place, contains interesting fishing-related displays, and the Peter Anson collection of paintings of fishing villages. Timber boat building still survives in Commercial Road. Many of the fishermen of Buckie shared the same name (e.g. Cowie), which required the use of Tee-names or nicknames. These were recorded in **Fishing Boats and Fisher folk on the East Coast of Scotland** by the artist Peter Anson (1930) and included: Dozie, Bo, Pendy, Bodger, Shakes and Fosky.

aspirations with a striking, open crown spire. Across the Square, **All Saints** Episcopal, 1875, by Alexander Ross is a neat gabled design with a stone broach spire. The **Commercial Hotel,** High Street, has two finely carved entrances, one with a pediment, the other a cornice, held up by scrolled brackets. **St Peter's,** 1857, designed by the Rt. Rev. James Kyle and Alexander Ellis, and closing the vista along St Peter's Road, symbolises the respectability achieved by Banffshire's Catholics after their legalisation in 1829. It has an imposing, twin-towered west facade (not unlike Armagh) and an elegantly traceried Gothic west front. The houses and hotel facing it comprise one of the nicest and least windswept corners of Victorian Buckie. In South West Street can be found a simple, stone, flat-roofed, 1930s police station.

On the shore, Buckie, Seatown and Yardie lie east of the Burn, and Buckpool west of it linked together by the curving **Great Western Road.** The older houses are to be found in Bridge End and Bowde's Lane. The houses facing Main Street, and the lanes going down to the former harbour are grander. Most are two-storey, or are cottages with an attic dormered storey. Originally, the upper storeys were lofts used for nets, usually entered from outside staircases, but most have now been converted into further bedrooms. These cottages represent care and self-respect: many are brightly painted, and most are embellished with some architectural feature such as pedimented dormer windows. **Yardie,** swinging out round the promontory, retains fairly complete, well maintained and painted banks of houses and cottages, tightly

cramped together in little strips between road and shingle. No. **40** is dated 1851.

139 **Portessie,** originally Rottinslough, became a fishing station in 1727, but had neither pier nor harbour, the boats being pulled up on the shingle until they began to work out of Buckie. Most of the cottages sheltering between bluff and shingle are probably 19th century, some of the best being in Findlater Street, Hope Street, and Rannas Place.

140 **Inchgower Distillery,** 1871
In a lovely setting by the Letter Burn (which provides its water) dominated by the Bin of Cullen, Inchgower is large quadrangular building with the usual roofscape, and good stone workmen's houses. The spring, on the other side of the road, is celebrated in a white, barrel-vaulted shrine.

Left: Portessie. **Top:** St Peter's Church. **Above:** Commercial Hotel. **Below and bottom:** Inchgower Distillery and its spring.

141 **Rathven**
Former centre of a large parish (and mediaeval leper colony) Rathven is now overtaken in importance by the seaside communities of Findochty and Portknockie. Set on a fairly high site, commanding wide views to the Bin Hill, to Speyside to the west, and down to Buckie, the **Church** is a simple white box kirk, 1794, with round headed windows, and a belfry. The old kirkyard some yards west, with

Of Rannas the seat of the Hays just to the south, only a wing and a walled garden survives. The most celebrated Hay was the *Jacobite Giant* the 7 ft. 2 ins. tall Andrew Hay (1713-89) who was a prominent figure in the '45, and accompanied Bonnie Prince Charlie on the march to Derby. His notoriety made it impossible for him to return to his patrimony until 1763, having spent six years as a fugitive in Scotland and a further 11 on the Continent. His sister Mary had married John Leith of Leith Hall in Aberdeenshire in 1730. Hay's brother-in-law died in 1736, and his nephew, also John, was shot in 1763, the year of his return. He offered support and encouragement to his neice, and in 1789 sold his own estate of Rannas, to purchase Leith Hall free of its growing debts, and returned it unencumbered to his great nephew Sandie, on the condition that the name Hay be added to Leith. Sandie subsequently became General Alexander Leith-Hay of Rannas and Leith Hall.

vestiges of walls and tombs, contains the Rannas Burial Aisle, 1612; a survival of the old kirk without distinguishing feature save the memorial slab of the Hays of nearby Rannas.

142 **Presholme,** 1788, Father John Reid, sanctuary by Peter Paul Pugin, 1896
Well worth the detour. Something of a Catholic shrine high on the hillside overlooking Buckie, attached to a Presbytery, a garden, a row of trees and now little else. The recently demolished *fermtoun* was an 1829 replacement of the heather-thatched row of cottages which formed the headquarters of the Catholic Church in Scotland from 1697 to 1878. The facade is a Scots echo of Italian baroque in stone and harl. It is the second oldest Roman Catholic church in Scotland, (St Ninian's at Tynet being its predecessor) and the first to be overtly purpose-built since the Reformation.

143 **Letterfourie House,** 1773, Robert Adam
Unusually tall and plain house for Adam, in a gorgeous setting. It consists of a cubic main block with two-storey wings entered through a rare Corinthian columned porch. Architraves and blind balustraded aprons at the three principal windows. From the garden, with its water and fountains, it presents four full, somewhat gaunt, storeys. The Granary, 1779, is harled, with a coat of arms and belfry. **Craigmin Bridge,** of similar date, is a wildly picturesque, two-storeyed, wavy-parapeted practical folly.

Top right: Rathven Kirk from the old kirkyard.
Above: Presholme.

Walkerdales Farm, 1677
One of three fairly grand farmhouses of the neighbourhood, with crowstep gables and an armorial panel. **Thornybank,** c. 1700, is a degree down the scale, plain harled with a projecting turnpike staircase. **Greenbank,** late 18th century, is a large, harled T-plan house with a contemporary circular doocot. **Cairnfield House,** 1802, another Gordon seat and rather grandly florid for this location, is entered

RCAHMS

Moray Planning Dept

In April 1746 *the 21 white fishers in the three fishing boats at Findochty appeared before the court of regality of Ogilvie to pledge themselves not to engage in bad practices with the Rebels or disaffected persons, and to fairy no person whatever to the sea other than the crew belonging to the boat.*

through a Doric columned doorway in a projecting, pedimented bay, with a Venetian window above. A columned corridor leads to a wing.

144 **FINDOCHTY**

In 1568 the Ord family acquired the *Manor, port, customs and fisher lands* of Findochty, but its real growth as a port begins with the import by Thomas Ord of Findochty Castle of thirteen men and four boys of Fraserburgh to fish in 1716.

145   **Findochty Castle,** c. 15th century, at the end of a drained loch, has been an L-plan keep, the main hall as usual on the first floor above vaulted cellars. Finely moulded window and door details now eroded beyond recognition.

The port soon expanded with the white fish and herring trade, but is now confined mainly to pleasure boating. It is dominated by the **Church,** 1863, a white, simple Gothic box, high on the bluff of Long Head, acting as a beacon to fishermen. Houses in **Church Street** and Blantyre Street are late Victorian terraces, densely built against the wind. The older houses are down at harbour level, whether facing the Hythe to the west or **Sandy Creek,** to the east. They are typical of the coast: mostly stone built, single-

Left: Letterfourie House. **Above:** Craigmin Bridge. **Below:** Findochty Castle.

Forrest

Moray Planning Dept

Above: Findochty from the air.
Below: The Harbour.

storey (some with attic rooms) and brightly coloured. There are minor variations: some have pedimented lintels over doors and windows (e.g. Jubilee Terrace) some with grander dormer windows (e.g. Main Street), and most present their gable end, their sturdy

McKean

McKean

Findochty Church.

shoulder, to the sea. Broad Hythe harbour was completed by David Stevenson, 1882-84. Station Road, linking the cottages around the harbour to the now vanished railway, contains grander Victorian and later houses and bungalows.

146 PORTKNOCKIE

Clifftop fishing port, founded in 1677 in the lee of Greencastle Hill to the east (on which prehistoric remains have been discovered), a virtually sheer 50 ft. cliff dropping to the harbour and paddling pool below. Older cottages toward the edge of the cliff are the usual single-storey and attic, gable to the sea stone cottages, as in Reidhaven, New, and Victoria streets. Later Victorian streets, e.g. Park Street, have trimmer

McKean

McKean

Above: Portknockie harbour.
Left: Park Street, a fine line of captains' houses running down to the cliff.

1 Jubilee Terrace, Findochty — a good example of the grander Victorian fisher houses of this coast.

Moray Planning Dept.

stone houses with white painted margins to doors and windows, once the homes of skippers. The **County Library,** 1892, has pedimented dormer windows, and the Victoria Hotel a pedimented door. The **Seafield Church,** 1838, on the outskirts, a plain stone bellcoted box designed by William Robertson, has been converted to a house.

CULLEN

Old Cullen had a major church, a Tolbooth and school adjacent. Stand by the south gates of the Kirk, and you stand in the middle of what used to be the Old High Street, the Cross just by your left shoulder. The Burgh's Royal Charter was confirmed in 1455 by King James II, with the peculiarity that, until the 19th century, there was no provision for a Provost. After 1600, the Earls of Findlater moved their seat from Findlater to the present Cullen House, bringing a much closer interest in the Burgh's affairs. The 5th Earl introduced linen manufacture in 1748 which Thomas Pennant found flourishing 21 years later: *nearly fifty thousand pounds worth of trade there annually* on about a hundred looms. Yet the town was *mean;* and when, four years later, Boswell brought Dr Johnson on his trip to the Highlands, he found it *but a very small town and the houses mostly poor buildings.* The Earl's factor offered to guide the pair round the celebrated newly landscaped policies, but Johnson declined: *he had not come to Scotland to see fine places of which there are enough in England; but wild objects — mountains, waterfalls, peculiar manners; in short, things he had not seen before.* At the end of the 18th century, the burgh was in decline once more, unable to compete with the mechanisation of weaving. In 1804 the houses were *in general mean and ill-built, and the streets have an irregular and dirty appearance.* The Shambles was in ruins, and to a family of improvers like the Seafields, the situation on their doorstep had become intolerable.

CULLEN

The best situated and most openly designed of all the seatowns in Moray District, where wide streets sweep down a hillside overlooking Cullen Bay. The original Royal Burgh of Inverculan was probably located between Castle Hill and the mouth of the Cullen Burn. Sometime in the Middle Ages it moved to high land just east of Cullen House, laid out in a long single street parallel to the Burn on which the mills were located. From at least the 17th century the *seamen under the hill* inhabited a separate Fishertown down by the shore.

RCAHMS

In 1811 the Seafields commissioned a plan for a New Town by George MacWilliam (altered in 1817 by Peter Brown) on a steep hillside to the east of the castle policies above the Fishertown. The first house was built in 1820, on the east side of Seafield Street, at the exact point of the railway arch. Over the next nine years, the entire burgh was removed to the grid-iron town, leaving just the Church as a memorial. The hub of the new town is the **Square,** mostly designed by William Robertson from 1823, the grandeur somewhat diminished by lorries thundering down the main Banff/Elgin road which traverses it. The **Town Hall** and **Seafield Arms** Hotel form the grandest part,

McKean

Above: The 1811 plan for a New Town, on the hill above the existing Fishertown.
Right: The Seafield Arms and Town Hall.

128

McKean

occupying the south-east corner and much of Seafield Street. Save for the Town Hall on the corner, these buildings, harled with stone margins, have classical decorum and style. The extension flanking the carriage entrance, with its oversailing roof and ovoid bulls-eye windows, shows flair. The **Town Hall** entrance was up steps to a three-bay, two-storey ashlar corner, a stone coat of arms in the parapet above, and displays a close similarity in composition to the Seafield Baths in Leith by John Paterson. A similar, but less grand, building faces it across the street, its raised window margins implying that it, too, should be harled. The remainder of the Square and Seafield Street is much the same: two storeyed, regular houses, frequently with shops at ground floor. The harled **Clydesdale Bank,** on the north west corner of the Square, by James Matthews, 1866, keeps that discipline with added swagger in the bracketed pediment above the door, and bracketed architraves above the windows. The earlier buildings on Seafield

McKean

Top: The main street looking through the redundant railway arches down to the sea. **Above:** The Square. **Below:** The Square, Cullen Bay and Portknockie in the distance.

McKean

I

Above: The Market Cross. **Right:** Castle Street. **Below:** The Manse. **Bottom:** A brick-dressed railway arch, on almost the exact location of the first house in Cullen's new town.

Street below the viaduct are plainer and more Georgian in feeling. **Castle Street** is wildly steep, lined by single-storey and attic stone cottages with pleasing variety of detail. **Deskford Street,** a cul-de-sac since the railway, is less dramatic, but maintains the pleasant sense of scale. Throughout, there are splendid views east-west from one end of the town to the other down lanes and wynds, downhill to Seafield Street and uphill beyond. **Reidhaven Street** is flatter, some of the houses picked out in the local tradition of painted stone and high-relief rectangular pointing. The **Seafield Church,** by Duncan MacMillan, 1900, is elegantly Gothic with an adventurous carved doorway.

Dominating the town are the 1882-84 **Railway Viaducts** designed by P. M. Barnett, the one bisecting the town in two giant arches and the other crossing the Burn of Cullen in eight. Portions of the slender Gothic **Market Cross** previously stood in Old Cullen, and date from 1696.

    Grant Street leads from the Square to the Cullen House policies and contains some pleasant later Victorian buildings, including the 1857 Bank of Scotland by W. Henderson. **Seafield Place** comprises the better suburb: **The Neuk** is grand, **the Manse** by William Robertson, c. 1830, classical, and nos. **9** and **11** have considerable quality. **The Wakes** is a large pretty T-plan house with groups of chimneys, gables and mouldings in the Elizabethan style. **Cathay House,** 1861, to the south, is a white L-plan building with decorative gables and ranks of dormer windows, originally built for a tea-trader retired from China.

Seatown

Jammed between the foot of Castle Hill and the shingle, the Seatown may occupy the site of ancient Inverculan, *seamen under the hill* being recorded in 1617. Twenty-nine families were living in the Fishertown by 1762, some of whose squat cottages still survive. Virtually all Seatown houses are one-

McKean

storey with attic, huddled together in lines, a regiment of gables facing the shore. These wynds are traversed by a wandering central *street* running from one end to the other, parallel with Castle Terrace which severs the Seatown from the south. Characteristic decoration of fisherhouses, with the occasional embellishment: no. **74** has a corbelled oriel window, dormer windows and skewputts, no. **94** an 1868 datestone, no. **255** (dated 1760), the only full two-storey house, and no. **68** a cornice and fancy windows. The **Methodist Church,** 1900, is a respectable stone Gothic box dominating the houses by virtue of its bulk. The **Royal Oak** Hotel is picked out in white and blue, embellished with masonry dormer windows and skewputts. Cullen bay can attract ferocious waves, but a new sea wall and wide seafront road, built in 1953 after storms and severe flooding, has left the Seatown somewhat beached. The first formal **Harbour** is signalled by the 1736 payment of 5 guineas by the Earl of Findlater to William Adam for a plan. The current harbour was begun in 1817, rebuilt in 1823 and added to by William Robertson in 1834. The outer pier is constructed of beautifully cut ashlar blocks.

McKean

McKean

Top: The Seatown. **Middle:** Typical raised pointing. **Above:** The Seatown close-up, with parked boat. **Left:** Cullen from the sands.

McKean

A distinctive product of Cullen is Cullen Skink, a rich cream soup created from smoked haddock and other ingredients, excellent as a winter warmer.

The Glasgow Fair was a major event in the Cullen economy. In mid-July, Glaswegian holiday makers streamed out of Cullen station down into the town. Many poorer people — including fisher folk — were thus provided with a critical means of augmenting the annual income, for local Cullen families moved out of their houses to shacks at the bottom of the garden, bothies or other shelters: letting their houses to the incomers. From the 1960s, cheap flights to the sun probably seduced some of the holiday makers, and the closure of the railway was the last straw. Cullen and the Glasgow Fair now connect little. Some of the shacks at the bottom of the garden still survive: but holiday makers in Cullen nowadays are just as likely to own one of those old cottages as a second home.

148 **Old Kirk,** from 12th century

The church of St Mary of Cullen can be traced back at least to 1327, when King Robert the Bruce endowed *with mad mourning and woe* a chaplaincy for his wife Elizabeth, who died there. It is delightfully old Scots, completed to a cross plan, set within a well-tombed churchyard with high walls containing fine memorial slabs. Fairly plain from the outside, distinguished by a bellcote, a gable with four tall lancet windows, and outside stairs, the glory lies inside. Although retaining a romanesque arch within, the Church's chief attractions date from 1536 with the addition of St Anne's Aisle, erected by Helen Hay and John Duff of Muldavit; from 1543, when the Church was raised to Collegiate status by Alexander Ogilvy of Findlater; from 1554, when the outstanding rich, columned and canopied monument to Alexander Ogilvy was created; and from 1602 when the Findlaters built their imposing laird's loft (now called the Seafield Loft).

Top right: The outstanding 16th century Ogilvie monument in the Old Kirk. **Above:** the 17th century Seafield Loft. Note the carved uprights. **Below:** *A flying skeleton* in the kirkyard wall. **Below right:** The Old Kirk.

Left: Cullen House. Above: Findlater Castle in the 18th century. Little now survives.

Cullen House, from 1600

Upon the 20th day of March 1600, the Laird's house in Cullen was begun and the ground broken; thus the origins of what became one of the grandest houses in Scotland (after the 1858 additions extending to 386 rooms). Set high on a rock above the burn, the house probably incorporates material from older buildings, reputedly the residence of the prebendaries of the Collegiate Church. The oldest identifiable portion of this enormously complicated structure was probably a four storey tower in the south east corner on the edge of the cliff, each gable decorated with little corbelled turrets. The original doorway, splendidly decorated with roundels and exotically vegetarian pilasters, is now walled up as a window, immediately abutting the south wing. A florid, later 17th century stair tower is visible from the gorge below, known as the Punch Bowl.

Three-storey wings extending to west and north are probably contemporary, although some of the vaulted chambers may well be earlier. The dormer windows are carved with an exuberance little short of fantastic, and the two entrance doorways, east and west are graced with stonework very like that of the walled up

The Ogilvies of Findlater, whose ruined castle crowns a headland a few miles to the east of Cullen, arrived with the marriage of Sir Walter de Ogilvy of Auchlevan to the heiress of Sir John Sinclair of Deskford and Findlater in 1437. Although Findlater was a prominent castle, and Deskford (see p. 136) likewise, it is improbable that there was not also a town house or manor in Cullen itself, maybe on the Castle Hill. In 1482, the Ogilvies were granted the additional lands of Findochty and Seafield. Their accustomed parish church was at nearby Fordyce until 1543 when their patronage moved to Cullen.

Below: 1726 gravestone of the Hay family in the kirkyard. **Left:** Cullen House.

Above: Cullen House: views of the exterior, the extravagant dormer window, the principal entrance, and James Adam's splendid stair balustrade.
Below: William Adam's bridge and the Bin Hill, James Adam's *Grand Entrance*, and the *Temple of Fame* (or Pomona).

McKean

Left: The 17th century painted ceiling.

In 1545 Alexander Ogilvie alienated his entire property to his son-in-law Sir John Gordon, third son of the Marquis of Huntly at nearby Bog o' Gicht (see p. 114). His son James received it all back in 1562 save for Auchindoun (see p. 150). In 1600, work began on the present Cullen House, signifying the beginning of the end for Findlater. In 1645 the town and house were *pitiably plundered* by the Farquharsons of Braemar acting for Montrose, and in 1646 the General Assembly of Scotland recommended all presbyteries to donate the first two days collection from every church to alleviate the *distressed estate of the town of Cullen which was utterly brunt.* In 1616 Sir Walter Ogilvie had been created Lord Deskford, and in 1638 the Earl of Findlater. In 1701 James, son of the 3rd Earl, was created Earl of Seafield, succeeding to his father's title in addition in 1711. He was appointed Scottish Secretary of State, Solicitor General, and High Commissioner to the General Assembly. Originally in favour of the Union of Parliaments in 1707, his being the phrase: *There's an end to an auld sang,* he recanted later, and died in 1730. His son, one of the great 18th century estate improvers, brought industry, gardens and William Adam to Cullen. With the death of James, 7th Earl of Findlater in 1811, the line was succeeded, in the earldom of Seafield only, by Sir Lewis Alexander Grant.

doorway, with lion caryatids. The east wing was extended in 1711, although the Earl determined against the classical beauties of a scheme prepared by James Smith and Alexander McGill. Instead, the east front was extended with two four-storey pavilions whose regular ranks of windows and splendid staircase are probably from James Adam's hand, 1769. In 1859 Seafield brought David Bryce to homogenise the assembly which he did by a marvellous baronialising of the south west end, a baronial gable to balance at the north west, and some wonderful interiors, particularly the library. Of the earlier period, the most notable survivals were, until the recent tragic fire, a room with a 17th century coved timber ceiling, beautifully painted with allegorical scenes and the arms of Charles II; and the stairhall, with its delicate iron work of 100 years later.

After being abandoned by the Earls, in 1984-85 Cullen House was converted into 11 separate dwellings by Kit Martin with Douglas Forrest. The latter has created a galleried house from the old kitchen and an architectural studio from the old laundry.

Cullen House Policies

The Earls were anxious early to capitalise on the dramatic setting to create a landscape according to fashionable taste. William Adam provided the fine **West Bridge** in 1744; his son James the Grand Entrance, a pedimented, Doric columned gateway capped with a statue in 1767, the Ivy Bridge (also 18th century), and an ice house. The **Temple of Fame,** down by the sea was designed by James Playfair in 1788. A rotunda on eight Ionic columns, above a panelled room with an ingenious underfloor heating system, it was finally erected by William Robertson in 1822. The hollow square steading, on the west, is also 18th century.

Below: The Dower House.

RCAHMS

DESKFORD

Cullen Harbour in 1819

The fishing vessels are just come in, having caught about 300 barrels of herrings during the night. All hands were busy. Some in clearing from the nets the fish which were caught by the gills; some in shovelling them with a long and broad wooden shovel into baskets; women walked more than knee deep into the water to take these baskets on their backs, while under sheds erected for protection in hot weather, girls and women out of number were employed in ripping out the gills and entrails, some others in strewing salt over them, and others again in taking them from the troughs into which they were thrown after this operation, and packing them into barrels. Others were spreading the nets to dry. . . . Air and ocean also were alive with flocks of sea fowl, dipping every minute for their share in the herring fishery. . . . A heap of dog-fish was lying on the pier. . . . Robert Southey.

Top right: Deskford Castle in the 18th century. **Right:** Deskford Kirk. **Below:** The Ogilvie monument.

McKean

149 Deskford

A tiny, pretty village, shorn of its once considerable glory as a seat of the Ogilvies of Cullen and Deskford, later Earls of Findlater and Seafield. The grand 16th century four-storey **Tower** was demolished in the 1830s, although some of its palatial outbuilding survives. Ruins of the adjacent mediaeval **Church** are notable for the gorgeous 1551 Sacrament House and a tear-shaped monument to Walter Ogilvy, both beautifully carved in golden stone, and ogee-headed piscinas, all evidence of vanished eminence. The **Old Manse** (now Deskford House) dates from 1773, and the **Dominie,** an old schoolhouse near the Church was built c. 1800, as was Berryhillock Village and Mill just upstream. **Deskford Kirk** is a fairly elaborate, cruciform, isolated Gothic box kirk with a well composed west front.

Forrest

The lozenge-shaped stone declaims in Latin: *Mr Walter Ogilvy, a pious minister of the work of God, now one of the happy inhabitants of heaven, died 15 February 1658.*

Forrest

150 Grange Parish Church, 1795

Plain, rectangular box kirk recognising growth in this agricultural parish after its split from Keith in 1618, and built on the site of the *place of great splendour,* the Grange of the Abbots of Kinloss. A bright, pleasant, galleried interior. The **Bridge of Grange,** 1699, crosses the Isla. The Garrowood Hotel romantically clinging to the far side, is Victorian with a picturesque oddity across the yard. Braco House, a Victorian house of substance, recalls the Earls of Fife. Three communities on the east enjoy the names Nethertown of Knock, Knock, and the Yondertown of Knock.

Forrest

151 Edingight House, from 1559

Begun for John Innes as a two-storey harled laird's
block with a huge chimney and a forestair, it was
extended in 1615 by the 5th Innes Laird with a
fashionable mansion with skewputts, a hall in the
upper storey. The overmantel is dated 1681. Since
regularised, and reconditioned in 1955. The Lord
Lyon King of Arms is Innes of Edingight.

152 Milltown of Rothiemay

Set low in a bowl of hills at the very frontier of
ancient Aberdeenshire, Rothiemay is off most beaten
tracks. A beautiful, granite-built village winding down
to the Deveron river where were once set the Mills of
the Milltown of Rothiemay. The whinstone **Kirk**,
1807, is a plain, unharled box with belfry still
arranged in traditional Presbyterian fashion of galleries
and pews facing a pulpit in the centre of the south
wall. It is the successor to that officiated in by John
Gordon of Rothiemay, the celebrated cartographer
who produced the outstandingly valuable picture maps
of Aberdeen and Edinburgh during the years of the
Civil War in the 17th century. Only the foundations
of St Dunstan's survive, the remainder having been
cannibalised for the new erection. A baronial gateway
(1906) signifies the entrance to the vanished
Rothiemay Castle in a lovely setting above the
Deveron. The original 16th century Z-plan tower had
many similarities to Ballindalloch: a circular entrance

Forrest

Top left: Edingight. **Above:** The
1551 Sacrament House in Deskford
Kirk. **Below:** Rothiemay c. 1905.
Below left: Rothiemay Castle in
1951 (demolished), measured and
drawn by Alexander Mennie.

Alexander Mennie

Elgin Library

tower corbelled square at the top, with a projecting oriel window. It was extended in late 17th century Scots classical: a long, plain tall mansion block focussed on a semi-circular pediment with a bulls-eye. The Doocot, 18th century, is long rectangular, twin chambered and ruined. The Forbes Arms, beside the river is late 18th century plain, two-storey Georgian. Mill House is a mid 18th century cottage with stone dormer windows. The current Bridge, 1872, was designed by John Willet. **Queen Mary's Bridge** is pre-1562 (she is thought to have slept in Rothiemay also). The 17th century Barn had threshing and winnowing on the ground floor, a house above, and a granary above that. Rothiemay is now, as it was 150 years ago, dominated by the *beautiful rural scenery equalled by few and excelled by none of equal extent in the Kingdom.* There is some evidence that there may have been brewing if not distilling in 17th century Rothiemay and that the Rothiemay Kiln with its slated egg-shaped kiln barn, was built as a mash-house, with a still in the adjoining building.

153 Mayen House, 1788

The curiously rustic classical three-bay entrance front is the principal survivor of a large, cubic, late Georgian villa, hugely extended to the rear in the 19th century. It is composed, beneath a pavilion roof and twin chimney stacks, of the main entrance flanked by twin, two-storeyed blind arches, the upper with Venetian windows, the lower similar without the curve. The corners are quoined.

154 **Mains of Mayen,** from 1608, is chocolate-box picturesque: L-shaped, crowstepped, one-and-a-half-storeyed farmhouse, a circular stairtower in the heel with a witches' hat. The later wing has a crowstepped porch.

Top: Rothiemay Castle, south front. **Middle:** The Kirk. **Above:** Mains of Mayen. **Right:** Mayen House.

McKean

KEITH

155**Old Keith,** which can still be traced along the banks
of the river Isla, dates back to c. 700 when Maelrubha
came to Christianise. It later became a fief of the
Abbot of Kinloss, who used it as a centre for
agriculture, and for distilling. A long, thin working
town, it used to straggle along the east bank of the
Isla, from the 16th century Ogilvy seat Milton Tower,
at the north, down beyond the old Kirkyard. The
surviving **pack-horse bridge** was the sole way of
crossing the Isla on the main Aberdeen-Inverness
overland route, to which the old town also presented a
blockage. It was the location of a massive annual Fair,
and the site of the last successful Jacobite skirmish in
1746. It was in Keith that James McPherson was
captured by Willliam Duff of Braco, prior to his
hanging in Banff, celebrated by Burns' *McPherson's
Rant.* In 1750, the improving Earl of Seafield
dissolved the blockage by rationalising the community
into a grid-iron New Town on the gallows moor to
the east. The main Aberdeen/Inverness road, instead
of cutting across Keith on the short axis as before,
was diverted down the long axis, Moss Street, and
across the bottom of the enormous, continentally-
proportioned Reidhaven Square. Save through the
Square, the town was given no internal cross streets
wide enough for vehicles. Traces of the **Old Kirk**
remain on a mound rising above the Isla. There are
some excellent tombs. The superbly pedimented slab

Old Keith kirkyard and packhorse
bridge.

Tomb to Milne of Kinstair.

McKean

Strathisla Distillery.

to the Johnstons, possibly built in the old church wall, is flanked with Corinthian columns and graced with luxuriant heraldic devices. The 1754 Corinthian tomb of Milne of Kinstair is yet grander, a flying skeleton adorning the plinth. The **Auld Brig,** leading from the graveyard, was built for packhorses in 1609 by Thomas Murray and Janet Lindsay. The **Old Town** is commemorated by a steep, cottagey street leading north east to **St Rufus Kirk,** 1816-18, built in the flamboyantly perpendicular style associated with Gillespie Graham.

McKean

There comes Summer-Eve
The huge scale of Reidhaven Square is explained by the translation to it of the annual Summer-Eve Fair held each September. It was the greatest animal tryst in northern Scotland, from which much stock was driven south to Barnet. *To it the whole merchants of Aberdeen, leaving their shops almost empty, with all their goods repaired, and very little unsold was carried back. All the carriers and many of the smaller farmers in the vicinity were employed for 10 or 12 days before the market. They travelled in caravans, from a dozen to 40 together; their approach was announced with joy, when first descried upon the brow of the distant hill:* **There comes Summer Eve, and the foremost troop of the Packers.**

156 **Strathisla Distillery,** founded 1786

The position of the distillery is most romantic; a wood-crowned hill overtops it on the side, whilst the opposite side of the valley is ornamented with pretty villas whose grounds stretch down to the waters edge, and the old kirk on another hill looks serenely into the busy establishment below. Thus Alfred Barnard in 1886. So largely does it remain today. Originally built as the Milton Distillery in 1784 by George Taylor and Alexander Milne, it now consists of a large picturesque, mostly 19th century complex dominated by the pagoda vents of the kiln, installed in the 1870s. The water wheel was added in 1881 to drive the machinery, and drove the rummager until 1965. In the pretty, 19th century gable of the granary, are two heraldic stones from nearby Milton Tower, one commemorating Lady Margaret Ogilvy who added to the castle in 1600. Now owned by Chivas brothers, part of the House of Seagram, Strathisla is the centre of Chivas' northern operations. Open to the public.

Milton Tower, 16th century
Scant remains of a three-storey tower seat of the
Ogilvies who succeeded the Abbots of Kinloss as
principal feuars in the District after the Reformation.
It passed to the Oliphants in the late 17th century,
and fell into ruin in the next.

Below: Aerial view of Reidhaven
Square. **Bottom:** Mid Street and
the Institute.

157 NEW KEITH

Mid Street, the principal one, has a character similar
to new Buckie but for the saving grace that the scale
is much tighter. It is dominated by the clock tower of
the **Institute,** 1885-89, by F. D. Robertson — a
pretty Renaissance campanile, graceful enough to
lighten the seriousness of the rest. The **Commercial
Hotel** has a worthy Gothic doorway and lacy iron
crown on the roof. The exuberantly painted, wild
floral carving above the doors and windows, conceals
the fact that the **Seafield Arms** was built in 1762.
Most of the remainder of Mid Street is two-storey
early 19th century. Nos. **49** and **51,** 1850-56, are
Tudor in style, with mullions and octagonal chimneys.
North and Newmill Church, 1845-46, by A. and
W. Reid, is pleasantly Gothic, with a central tower,
buttresses, interlaced arcades and a moulded doorway.

Moss Street is plainer, but contains the Anglia
Building Society, twin Dutch gables, quoins, and balls
above the doorway; its neighbour, a shell-hood above
the door, with the same exuberantly floral carving
above the windows as the Seafield Arms; and the
grandly Elizabethan building on the corner of
Reidhaven Square with gables, string courses,
mullioned windows and grouped octagonal chimneys.

Right: Mid Street.

St John Ogilvie is the best known member of the family that occupied Milton Tower. Born at the Drum of Keith in 1580, John rejected the Protestantism of his family and, converted to Catholicism, spent many years in Europe. In 1614 he was to be found in Glasgow, a popular man by all accounts. Unfortunately, Archbishop Spottiswoode succumbed to pressure from King James in London for action against Catholics and the Ogilvie trial in 1615 was his token response. The charge was treason, and was upheld upon Ogilvie's confession that, if instructed, he would obey the Pope above the King. He was hanged the same day at Glasgow Cross. In 1976, he was elected to the sainthood of St John Ogilvie, the first Scottish saint since Malcolm Canmore's queen, Margaret. There is a memorial to him outside St Thomas' Church.

Below: Chapel Street and St Thomas' Church.

Land Street is more isolated. **Chapel House** has a pedimented entrance bay capped by an iron star, and curious details. A pair of semi-detached cottages boast brick dressings for an arcade of semi-circular windows. **Mansefield Hotel** is old Scots in its white painted gables and stone dressings.

Reidhaven Square, early 19th century, is somewhat reminiscent of Ancaster Square in Callander: two and one-storey cottages and houses, well mannered but insufficiently grand to enclose the space. It has the scale and proportion of a Continental market square, suitable for its purpose as the site of the great, annual Summer-Eve Fair. **Chapel Street,** at the head, which leads up to St Thomas Church, contains some good town houses — particularly nos. **7-9,** late 18th century, and the polished stone **Cuthill**

House with its fine, Doric-columned, pedimented doorway.

St Thomas R.C., 1831-1832
Possibly designed by Father Walter Lovi, St Thomas closes the Chapel Street vista with a fine, pedimented, pilastered, Italianate facade — the best in the area — surmounted by a bulbous, imposing dome added by Charles Menart in 1916. The original church was built with funds raised by Lovi on a European fund raising trip, during which King Charles X commissioned (and donated) the painting *The Incredulity of St Thomas* from Francois Dubois.

The austere early English **Holy Trinity** Episcopal, Seafield Avenue, was designed by Alexander Ross in 1882 amidst pleasantly wooded villas in an affluent new area of town. The road continues down to **Isla Bank Mills,** turreted and gabled in 1889, but a group of mainly 1805 mill buildings, still selling tweeds and woollens, and offering guided tours. Keith Junction Station, despite the removal of many of its buildings, retains the atmosphere of a country halt. Nearby **Glen Keith** Distillery, Station Road, was converted from a Meal Mill in 1958, the head of Seagram, Sam Bronfman, insisting that it matched the character of the neighbourhood. The nearby early 19th century Tannery retains its louvred ventilators.

Union Bridge, 1770, at a higher level than the pack horse bridge (in keeping with the aspiration of the new town) was built over Gaun's Pool, in which the folk of Keith had the custom of drowning suspected witches.

Top: House, Moss Street. **Middle:** Stone house with brick dressings in Land Street. **Above:** St Rufus' Kirk. **Left:** Fife Keith.

158 **Fife Keith,** founded in 1817 by the Earl of Fife on the west bank of the Isla, is similarly grid-planned around **Regent Square** (disfigured, like Fochabers by a bus shelter and lavatory). No churches, however; the

only building of prominence is the former **Inn,** (now flats), no. 47 Regent Street, 1817, with its pedimented ashlar central bay, ball finial, and columned doorway the wings now harled. The remainder of the street and square is contemporary, although the scale is much wider than in the rival across the Isla, and lacks its containment.

Newmill in the '20s.

Auchroisk Distillery.

159 **Newmill,** looking like a miniature Dufftown, was established as a rival to new Keith by the Earls of Fife, c. 1759, adjacent to *an old little village* of that name. Like all such plantations, but most similar to Archiestown, it consists of a main street leading into a central square, dominated by the 1923 War Memorial clock tower and decaying Art-Deco garage. A Gothic church lies just to the east. By 1798 it consisted of *poor people who have settled there for the accommodation of peat fuel and a small croft of land.* A 19th century Mill survives, the usual two-storey rectangle with a wooden vent.

Crooks Mill, an 1895 L-plan rubble building, retains its kiln, its iron wheel (unused) and three pairs of millstones. **Glentauchers Distillery,** 1898, is tall and plain, with the usual pair of pagoda vents. **Edintore House** is a substantial 1840 mansion and Pitlurg Castle the vaulted ruin of a late 16th century tower.

The original 1696 portion of **Mains of Mulben** is concealed beneath a T-plan, Victorian, crowstepped farm. **Auchroisk Distillery,** 1973, by Westminster Design Associates, one of the most elegant of all the 20th century distilleries, is plain white and black, a conical yeast house and a jagged roof profile, in beautifully landscaped surroundings. **Auchlunkart House,** 1700, was, in 1798, *improved into the elegance of modern fashion with the convenience of a kitchen garden and the shelter of a little grove,* and given a Grecian porte-cochère in 1834. **Boharm Parish Church,** built in 1793 *pretty central to the parish* to

144

replace the *old fabrick* three miles south west, is now an agricultural store. The tall **Manse,** 1811, (now House of Boharm) stands below the Church, with a forestair and new, but appropriate, classical doorway, fanlight, and garden.

160 **Boharm** (or Gauldwell/Galival/Bucharin) **Castle,** c. 13th century
Apart from the fact that the *Castellum de Bucharin* belonged to the Freskyns of Moravia in 1200, little is known. High on a bluff above the Fiddich, sufficient survived in 1798 that it could be surveyed for the **Muckle Isaac:** *a large pile that fronted east and measured inside the walls 119 ft. by 24 ft. Fifty years ago, the walls were tolerably entire to the height of several storeys . . . they were eight feet thick and built in frames and grounded with lime mortar.* It was probably a massive hall-house.

Mill of Towie, is a c. 1800 meal-mill restored by Douglas Forrest as a restaurant with play area. The mill has a projecting kiln and an excellent 14 ft. diameter wood and iron waterwheel. Towiemore Distillery, now inoperative, was built in 1898 and consists of a large range of bonded stores and twin
161 kilns. **Botriphnie Parish Church** was built in 1820 on an ancient site dedicated to Fumac, replacing a 17th century church whose remains were purloined by the Duffs of Drummuir for a mausoleum. The bell of this pretty building with its round-headed windows, was cast in 1753 by John Mowat.

Boharm Castle in the 18th century.

The Old Parish Church by Maggieknockater, whose belfry once held a 1658 Cowie bell, was probably built after the remote chapels of this wild place — Nicholas Chapel, Boat o' Brig, Galvall Castle, and Arndilly were united in 1618 to form Boharm. Even after the amalgamation, the parish remained poor. In 1798 the school had *not been in a flourishing state for many years; a sorry cottage is uncommodiously situated behind the old church. The salary is only a wretched pittance £5:4:0d., about half the wages of an ordinary farm servant.*

Botriphnie Kirk.

162 **Drummuir Castle,** Thomas Mackenzie, 1847
The Duff connection with Drummuir began with its purchase by Adam Duff in 1670. The original house was superseded c. 1700 by Kirkton House — *a little log cabin in the woods* replaced in its turn by the grand mansion commissioned by Admiral Duff in 1847. Mackenzie gave his client the castellated grandeur he required: castellated towers at each corner, a Gothic

St Fumac's Well beside the church, used to contain a wooden effigy of the Saint, which was ritualistically washed annually on 3rd May, St Fumac's Fair.

K

DRUMMUIR

Drummuir did not retain its popularity for long. In 1908, its owner Thomas Gordon Duff compiled a defects schedule to justify demolition:

1st: The roof catches the snow and rain and it is very difficult to keep out water, almost impossible.

2nd: It is very difficult to warm. The centre space is **too** great.

3rd: The chance of fire is terrible. If fire did once catch hold it would be gone in an hour.

4th: The arrangement of the hall and rooms is such that sounds are heard all over — that it is difficult to get in a lift or another bathroom or modern wants — that it requires scaffolding to get at the central hall walls to clean them.

5th: It requires a lot of servants owing to the length of passages, etc.

The only merits are that the rooms are lofty and light and that the staircase is good.

In my opinion, it is a somewhat vulgar pretentious house, and is far too big for the estate, which is steadily diminishing in value, while costs of living as steadily increase, (owing to rise in wages). It will be, I fear, a serious problem for my son some day what to do with it. I do not think its faults can be remedied unless at **great** cost. And, such as the unsatisfactory of the fabric would not justify. It ought to be pulled down and a house suitable to the climate of the pocket of the owner built.

Top and below: Drummuir House.
Right: Hazelwood.

Forrest

Forrest

porte-cochère at the entrance; grand rooms with elaborate plasterwork and delicately Gothicised doors inside, including an unusual central lightwell in plasterer's Gothic. Currently under restoration by Douglas Forrest. The early 17th century remains of Drummuir farm three miles east was the early centre of the Drummuir lands.

The lower **Fiddich** is wild and beautiful below Balvenie. Not unlike a miniature Balmoral, **Buchromb,** 1873, was a grand baronial transformation of an earlier house, of which little

163 survives. **Hazelwood** is the converse: a classical, single-storey mansion in the manner of Archibald Simpson, with an oversailing roof, pedimented, pilastered porch and grouped chimneys.

164 **Kininvie,** the seat of the Leslies of Kininvie since 1480, presents a tall, 16th century white, narrow L-plan tower with re-entrant circular stair tower survives. *This commodious inhabitation of his very remote ancestors* failed to satisfy James Leslie, who had William Robertson extend it prettily in 1840.

RCAHMS

165 **Balvenie Castle,** from 13th century
An early fortified site commanding the passes into Moray from Huntly to the east, the Cabrach to the south, and Glen Rinnes to the west. It became a stronghold of the Comyns who were probably responsible for the huge stone curtain wall standing

McKean

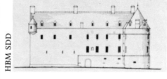

HBM SDD

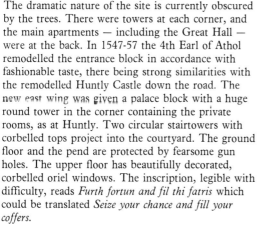

McKean

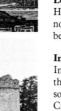

Left: Balvenie Castle (and New House) in the 18th century, and now. **Above:** as it might have been.

In 1615 Balvenie passed to the Inneses of Innermarkie, related to those of Coxton, and involved in a sordid murder of the Innes of Cromy, (heir to house of Innes), in Aberdeen. In 1644, the castle was last used militarily by the Marquis of Montrose. Alexander Duff of Braco came into possession in 1687 and in 1722 his son William, Lord Braco, commissioned James Gibbs to design the New House across the valley. This austere but sophisticated building lasted until 1929.

Below: Kininvie. **Bottom:** Buchromb. **Bottom left:** Balvenie New House.

on a battered base, surrounded by a revetted ditch. The dramatic nature of the site is currently obscured by the trees. There were towers at each corner, and the main apartments — including the Great Hall — were at the back. In 1547-57 the 4th Earl of Athol remodelled the entrance block in accordance with fashionable taste, there being strong similarities with the remodelled Huntly Castle down the road. The new east wing was given a palace block with a huge round tower in the corner containing the private rooms, as at Huntly. Two circular stairtowers with corbelled tops project into the courtyard. The ground floor and the pend are protected by fearsome gun holes. The upper floor has beautifully decorated, corbelled oriel windows. The inscription, legible with difficulty, reads *Furth fortun and fil thi fatris* which could be translated *Seize your chance and fill your coffers.*

RCAHMS

RCAHMS

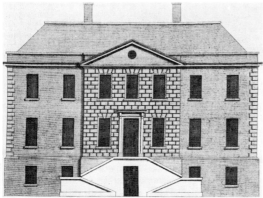

RCAHMS

McKean

Elgin Library

At the floor of the hill nestles the picturesque
166 **Glenfiddich Distillery,** founded in 1887 by William
Grant, formerly of nearby Mortlach Distillery, who
bought superannuated stills and equipment from
Cardow Distillery. In 1892 he bought more second-
hand equipment from Lagavulin (Isla) to open a
second distillery, **Balvenie,** cannibalising the Gibbs
mansion in the process. Visitor centre: tours.

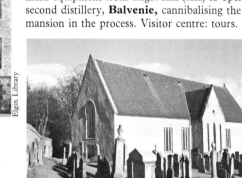

RCAHMS

Top: Glenfiddich Distillery.
Above: Balvenie New House.
Right: Mortlach Kirk. **Below:**
The monument to the Duffs of
Keithmore.

167 **Mortlach**
This lovely site above the Dullan Water has long been
a religious site, as its name (that of St Moluag of
Lismore) implies. Unconfirmed stories by Hector
Boece locate three Aberdeen bishops at Mortlach prior
to moving to Old Aberdeen. The **Parish Church** is a
large, 13th century, aisleless rectangle extended north
and south in 1826 and 1876. The east and west gables
retain original windows; the south elevation has pretty
20th century neo-Tudor windows and a projecting
early English gable. The north was drastically re-
mediaevalised in 1931. Inside, it is gracious but plain,
save for stones and monuments. The rather damaged
wall tomb of a knight in armour is thought to be that
of Alexander Leslie of Kininvie, c. 1549. On the
opposite wall is a superbly rustic baroque monument
to Alexander Duff of Keithmore and his wife Helen
Grant carved by John Faid in 1694. An odd broken
(but mended) grave slab in the porch is to the same

McKean

people. Beside it stands a finely carved stone with a Pictish beast and rare curvilinear symbol. There is an interesting early 19th century Watchhouse in the Kirkyard, and the tall **Battle Stone** said to commemorate the final defeat of the Danes in the district by Malcolm Canmore.

Danesfield (the former Manse), 1844, by Thomas Mackenzie, is prettily Tudor with grouped chimneys, mouldings and crumbling dormer windows. **Dufftown Glenlivet** distillery, just up the Dullan Water is an attractive 1896 distillery of low stone buildings. **Mortlach** distillery downstream toward the town, is a large traditional distillery, c. 1823. **Pittyvaich** House, 1750, is pleasantly old fashioned with crowstepped gables.

Above: Danesfield.
Below: Dufftown.

168 **Dufftown,** from 1817

Dufftown, founded by the Earl of Fife to alleviate unemployment after the Napoleonic Wars, is curiously laid out on an east-west axis, its square and tower as focus where its two main streets intersect. The **Clock Tower,** completed 1839 for use as the Jail and Burgh Chambers, is now used for Tourist Information. The clock came from Banff where, allegedly, it had been used (advanced an hour) to hang James McPherson (he of the rant). Vigorous, string coursed, turreted and bellcoted, the tower gives this predominantly two-storey, early 19th century town a visual focus. **Fife Street,** curving downhill, contains the pretty **St Mary's,** 1842, by James Kyle, a classical building with Gothic trimmings and a ribbed plaster vault inside, and **Dullanbrae,** c. 1840, an interesting villa in the harled, Elizabethan manner with an oriel window.

Strathcona and Mountstephen

Two Moray cousins, Donald Smith and George Stephen, were responsible for the opening up of much of Canada. Stephen was born son of a carpenter in Dufftown in 1829, and Smith in a little cottage by the Mosset Burn, Forres, in 1820. Both became involved in trade development and the construction of railways in Canada. Stephen became President of the Canadian Pacific Railway for which he and his cousin were primarily responsible. On their return, Stephen became Lord Mountstephen, and Smith Lord Strathcona. Mountstephen founded a hospital in Dufftown (as well as others elsewhere) and Strathcona the Leanchoil Hospital in Forres.

Balvenie Street contains a number of Victorian buildings aggrandised by crowstepped pediments and dormer windows. The **Clydesdale Bank,** c. 1880, is two-storey in expensive banker's classical, a consoled architrave dignifying the door. The Gothic revival **St Michael's** Episcopal, Conval Street, was designed 1880-1881 by Alexander Ross.

Church Street is perhaps the most interesting as it curves down to Mortlach. The pedimented **Picture House Cafe** is to what the Old Town Hall has risen. Further down Church Street toward Mortlach, an unusual Edwardian villa with tile-hung central bay projecting over porch.

Top: St Mary's Church. **Above:** The Tower. **Right:** Auchindoun Castle in the 18th century.

169 **Auchindoun Castle,** 15th century

A great craggy ruin on a hilltop above the Fiddich, burnt out in 1592 to revenge the murder of the Bonnie Earl of Moray by the Marquis of Huntly. Auchindoun consists of the shattered ruins of a tall tower with a rib-vaulted principal storey, enclosed by an outer, earlier, curtain-wall. In the 18th century, sufficient survived for it to be described *well finished in the Gothic style, several pairs of fluted pilasters raised in freestone are spread out in branches above their capitals . . . much of the appearance of a Gothic church.*

The **Mill** of Auchindoun, a ruinous L-plan mill with decayed timber vent was the site of a busy co-operative of illicit distillers in Edwardian times; only rumbled by the Excise after clyping by one who grudged his share of the profits. **Keithmore Farm** has a 1690 date stone in the steading.

Rome was founded on seven hills: Dufftown on seven stills (or so it was sung): Balvenie (1890), Dufftown Glenlivet (1896), Glendullan (1897), Glenfiddich (1887), Mortlach (1823 — the oldest by far preserving much of that atmosphere), Convalmore (1869), and Parkmore, now a store, replaced by Pittyvaich (1973).

Left: Cabrach Church.

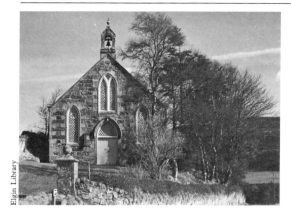

Elgin Library

170 The Cabrach

A once celebrated pony whisky route across a bleak
upland plateau guarded at the north by Auchindoun,
and the south by Auchindoir. It is the watershed of
the River Deveron. The **Parish Church,** along with
the graveyard wall and gates, dates from 1786. The
Manse, 1802, is plain regency, and the bridge over the
Allt Deveron, 1820. The pretty Gothic **Lower
Church,** 1873, was originally U.P., consolidating the
long Cabrach traditions of Secession. Nearby
Aldivalloch is commemorated in the song *Roy's Wife
of Aldivalloch* written by Mrs Grant of Carron. The
ruined **Mill of Corinacy,** 18th century, explains the
name Milltown. The Inn at Inverharroch is plain,
two-storey, c. 18th century, extended, on a bluff above
the Deveron.

The road south west from Dufftown to Glenlivet
passes through Glen Rinnes, a desolate but beautiful
spot *where there is never occasion to complain for want
of rain.* The 18th century **Mill of Laggan,** now used
as a shed, is wheel-less, one-storey and attic rubble.
Allt a' Bhainne distillery was designed in 1975 by
William Nimmo and Partners, a series of harled and
slated geometrical shapes cut into the hillside.

Messrs Chivas

Adam Gordon of Auchindoun
was brother to the Earl of Huntly,
and associated with the Catholic
faction during the reign of Queen
Mary and her successor, the
Regent Earl of Moray. Moray
invited the Master of Forbes to
suppress Gordon's activities on
behalf of the Queen, which he did
with little success at both
Tulliangus and Crabstane in late
1571. In revenge, Edom o' Gordon,
as he became known, either
personally or through a lieutenant,
a Captain Kerr, invested Corgarff
(at the other end of the Lecht)
burning Margaret Campbell,
Forbes' wife, children and
retainers:

> It fell about the Martinmas
> When the wind blew shrill and
>   cauld
> Said Edom o' Gordon to his
>   men
> We maun draw to a hauld.

The remainder of this grim ballad
(not one of the best of such)
outlines the consequence.

Roy's wife of Aldivalloch is an
odd song for a lady to have written,
being the lament of a young man
whose love has married an older
man with property:

> Roy's wife of Aldivalloch, Roy's
>   wife of Aldivalloch,
> Wat ye how she cheated me as
>   I cam' o'er the braes o'
>   Balloch?
> She vow'd, she swore she
>   would be mine; she said she
>   lo'ed me best o' onie;
> O the fickle, faithless quean,
>   she's ta'en the carl, and left
>   her Johnnie.
> O she was a cantie quean, well
>   could she dance the
>   Highland walloch
> How happy had she been mine,
>   or I been Roy of
>   Aldivalloch.

Left: Allt a' Bhainne Distillery.

Right: Orton House. **Above:** Boat of Brig.

THE SPEY VALLEY

The lower Spey Valley is narrow but fertile, squeezed between the Teindland and Ordiequish. Views from Aultderg past the Earth Pillars up to the hills beyond are of exceptional beauty (see p. 89).

171 **Dipple,** from 1675

A mainly 19th century harled, gabled, and skewputted farm with a square and laundry; basking in the reflected glory of its 1684 purchaser William Duff. The Steading, c. 1800, is a large, harled square, and the two-storey **Dairy,** with its pyramid roof, contains its original cheese-making equipment. Old Dipple Kirk was located in the circular graveyard nearby.

172 **Orton House,** 1786

Tall cubic classical house, in proportion not unlike Pitgaveny, ennobled by a pedimented, quoined three storey central bay, and a gigantic, balustraded Tuscan porte-cochère added by William Robertson in 1826. The three main bedrooms were on the ground floor, to allow the first floor to be occupied by *a magnificent suite of rooms* and the second floor by a library.

173 **Boat of Brig**

Like Boat of Bog, further north, the name perpetuates an ancient ferry across the Spey, which explains the pompous little pedimented, Tuscan columned *Pontage House* built in 1830 by William Robertson. The 1956 road bridge replaced a pretty Suspension Bridge, 1831-32, by Samuel Brown.

Dipple Dairy.

McKean

ROTHES

Founded in its present form by the Earl of Findlater as a crofting township in 1766. Each tenement was given 1/8 acre at an annual rent of 10/−. The poet laureate, Robert Southey, liked the *neatly built cottages of one floor each* in 1819, but disliked their *mournful uniformity*. It is now dependent upon distilleries and an animal feed factory.

Rothes Castle, 15th century
Barely a wall survives of the seat of the Leslies, Earls of Rothes. It consisted of a fortified plateau enclosing a hall-house protected by a drawbridge. Burnt by an Innes Covenanter, it was largely demolished, c. 1660, by the local inhabitants *to prevent its continuing to be a retreat of thieves and bandits who pillaged the neighbouring estates*. The Leslies moved to their new Palace by Glenrothes in Fife.

Rothes Kirk, 1781
A simple Georgian box Kirk with rounded windows, a steeple added to the west gable in 1870, to accommodate the donation of Nairn's former town clock.

RCAHMS

Top: Rothes. **Above:** Rothes Castle. **Below:** Hotel, New Street. **Below left:** Speyburn Distillery.

Elgin Library

RCAHMS

Above: Glen Grant Distillery.

The principal trade of Rothes wrote Alfred Barnard in 1887 *is whisky making, for which the water from the neighbouring hill seems peculiarly adapted.* Its first Distillery was Glen Grant, established by James and John Grant in 1840 and extended since then. It has the usual atmosphere of large rustic buildings. Glen Rothes was next, founded in 1878 by a group of local businessmen, followed by Glen Spey, founded in 1885 by James Stewart. Speyburn, attractively designed by the Elgin distillery architect Charles Doig arrived in 1897, as did Caperdonich — originally built as a massive annexe to Glen Grant, although now independent. Glen Grant has a visitors' centre, and offers tours.

Below: Glen Grant House. **Right:** Rothes Glen Hotel.

Old Rothes ran east-west along the banks of the burn. The dog-legged new town, running north/south, has a different feel: that of a lowland industrial town. To enjoy Rothes, you have to go beyond the main road. Around the Burnside are some of the grander civic buildings, as well as some of the older ones gable end to the street. The public buildings evince a muscular Victorianism, as in the **Town Hall** (now a community centre), 1898, by R. B. Pratt, now bereft of the Scots renaissance turrets that used to lighten it, and in the **Seafield Arms,** rebuilt with gable, roundel and finial in the 1880s. The **Free Church** (now a Church Hall), 1900, was possibly the grandest church in town, its broach spire, with roundels and trefoils somewhat more graceful than the establishment across the road. Some pleasant plain houses along Burnside. **Glen Grant House,** c. 1885, is engagingly hybrid — crowstep gables, decorative dormers, French towers and Elizabethan bay window.

Auchinroath, up the glen of Rothes, is a 1746 cottage substantially extended in baronial style. The **Rothes Glen Hotel** replaced a burnt 1871 summer house of the Dunbars with the wonderful, towered Scots baronial confection it is now, designed in 1893 by Alexander Ross. **Coleburn Distillery,** 1896, briefly glimpsed from the main road, is dominated by a large malt barn with a pagoda roof. **Millbuies Estate** lies on the divide between upland Speyside and the lowland Laich, and offers walks and nature trails of great interest. Nearer Elgin, **Longmorn** (1895) and **Benriach** (1898) distilleries can be seen, the latter one of the few operating floor maltings left in Scotland.

¹⁷⁵**Arndilly,** 1750

This *magnificent modern house* with its courtyard of lower buildings and extensive plantations, was built for David Macdowall Grant, enlarged in 1850 in the fashionable neo-Jacobean style by Thomas Mackenzie. It is a most romantic confection, with a balustraded porte-cochère, flights of steps and terraces, and a carved stone with both Pictish and Celtic symbols built into the west gable.

SPEY — NORTH BANK

176 **Easter Elchies,** 1700

Macallan (St Colin) was an independent parish until c. 1580 when it was joined to Knockando. By 1843 the kirkyard had become *rural and sequestered, with a fragment of the church wall still visible but mouldering away.* All that really survives is the Mausoleum for the Grants of Easter Elchies, the 1715 Wall Monument to John Grant dignified by Corinthian columns, a skull, high relief crossbones, and flying skeleton. The recent restoration of **Easter Elchies** for The Macallan by Michael Laird and Partners won a Civic Trust Award. The house was stripped of its Victorian accretions, and reverted to a tall, L-plan, crowstepped house of great dignity, with a single-storey low-set hexagonal extension. Its near cousin — the extended crowstepped 1681 Wester Elchies house for a Grant relative has been demolished.

Moray Planning Dept

Above: Arndilly. **Below:** Easter Elchies mausoleum in the Macallan graveyard. **Left:** Easter Elchies.

RCAHMS

Michael Laird

177 **Archiestown**

Founded in 1760 by Sir Archibald Grant of Monymusk as a way of improving the bleak Moor of Ballintomb, Archiestown is the only proper village in the parish. Conforming to normal plantation pattern, it consists of a principal street runnning through a square, with several by-lanes running off.

Archiestown took a long time to settle, hampered by a disastrous fire in 1783. It has, wrote the chronicler in 1798 *for several years been rather retrograde; the roads, only formed, not completed, have fallen into so much disrepair that to a wheel carriage the village is only accessible from the east. . . . By an accidental fire, some years ago, many of the houses were consumed, and their naked roofless walls suggest the idea of Tadmor in the desert or some other eastern city, on which judgment denounced by some ancient prophet hath in part been accomplished.*

Archiestown.

Elgin Library

McKean

RCAHMS

RCAHMS

Top: The view from Ballintomb over to Ben Rinnes. **Middle:** Knockando House. **Above:** Knockando Church.

The streets are well built with cottages and houses, and the Square has the **Hotel,** (1900), the Speyside weavers, and some of the better houses, the best of which is the pretty, harled **Free Church Manse,** with its columned doorway and central pediment; and the similar Old St Andrews, across the road, in its multi-coloured Ben Rinnes granite and original windows. Nearby Ladycroft Farm Museum offers a good collection of farm bye-gones, tea if required, and a superlative view over to Ben Rinnes. **The Cottage,** 1790, is a grand, single-storey laird's house in Rinnes granite with projecting wings, and ornamental railings on dwarf walls. Lord Strathcona's parents lived in this house.

178 **Knockando,** beautifully situated on the banks of the Spey, is a pleasantly old fashioned Scot U-plan house — its projecting entrance bay graced with quoins and a pediment capped by stone pinnacles. The nearby doocot, 17th century is crowstepped with two rat ledges. **Knockando Kirk** was a harled Georgian box, of 1757, with two outside stairs, until 1906 when a wholly new south front with twin Gothic gables and a French round tower were added. Built into the churchyard wall are three weathered, Pictish stones.

Knockando Station, a pretty white clapboard building, is now used as a visitor's centre for Tamdhu, an interesting building of post-war vintage. The Woollen Mill, c. 1800, has some of the oldest working machinery in the U.K., and is a working museum, weaving the white woollen habits for the monks at Pluscarden. **Knockando Distillery,** 1898, was the first to have electric light. The pagoda roofs of **Cardow** peep above ploughed fields although on closer inspection it appears more like the factory it is. Developed from 1824 as a diversification by the Cumming farmers of Cardow, in buildings *of the most straggling and primitive description* it was rebuilt in the boom years of 1884-85.

Elgin Library

179 **CRAIGELLACHIE**

Uphill, a largely Victorian hillside town, dramatically situated on a peninsula at the confluence of the Spey and the Fiddich. At river level, a picturesque street of older buildings leading to the gabled Craigellachie Hotel, designed by Charles Doig in 1892 in hunting lodge style. The upper town post-dates 1880, and consists of pleasant stone villas, worthy schools and churches, and the White Horse, Craigellachie Distillery on the plateau above, with interesting 1930-50 buildings. A rare cooperage alongside. The view up the Spey from Tunnel Brae known as the Queen's View is worth a detour.

180 **Craigellachie Bridge,** Thomas Telford, 1814

A lacy, gently bowed, and immensely graceful cast-iron single iron arch at a narrows where the Spey is at its most menacing, which transformed communications in this part of Scotland. The metal work was cast at Ruabon, North Wales and brought to Moray by sea. The rubbly castellated abutments were designed by Telford's assistant John Simpson. A mound and a further blind arch to the south were swept away in the Muckle Spate in 1829. The whole cost £8,200 and, is probably the oldest surviving iron bridge in Scotland. It is certainly the most impressive of that period. It was by-passed in 1972.

Craigellachie from the west.

Below: Craigellachie Hotel.
Bottom: Thomas Telford's celebrated Craigellachie Bridge.

Elgin Library

RCAHMS

Above: Ruins of St Drostan's kirk, the lacy ironwork of Victoria Bridge just peeping out behind. **Below:** The pack-horse bridge. **Bottom:** The Parish Church.

181 CHARLESTOWN OF ABERLOUR

The ancient community of Skirdustan consisted of a church, manse, some cottages and a schoolhouse beside St Drostan's Kirk, at the mouth of the Lour Burn (hence Aberlour). Some scant remains of the church survive in the beautiful graveyard beside the **Pack Horse Bridge** (repaired for £5 by mason Robert Duff in 1729), at the far west end of the current community. The elegantly plain classical house on the bluff above the burn is the **Old Manse** c. 1840. At the bottom of the graveyard is the lacy structure of the 1902 steel suspension **Victoria Bridge** built by James Abernethy.

In 1812, the community was promoted to the dignity of a **new town** by Charles Grant of Wester Elchies who graced it with his own name (hence Charlestown), in emulation of his kinsman Sir Archibald Grant who had thus sought immortality in his foundation Archiestown. The standard plan of a long street straddling a main road, with a focus upon a Square, is followed here. Yet Aberlour has a distinct identity: the mile-long street is lined with trees, the scale is spacious, pace relaxing, and surroundings splendid. Here is the Spey at its more benign.

Buildings in **the High Street** are generally Victorian, in crisp well-cut stone, but without Victorian extravaganza, rarely more than two storeys tall. The white-harled **Aberlour Hotel,** c. 1800, has a shoulder facing into the Square which was probably laid out around it. It faces the cosmopolitan **Clydesdale Bank,** 1870s, by James Matthews, whose large gabled bay and pilastered doorway are justly calculated to inspire confidence in the Victorian sporting tourists for whom it was built. The **Lour Hotel** next door, is smaller and later: a touch of the hunting-lodge aesthetic. Across the road, a row of

pretty, stone, half-timbered gabled houses face the church. Uphill may be found pleasant villas with excellent views north, the 1897 stone Jacobean-style school and the **Fleming Institute.** Designed in 1889 by W. Reid, the Institute was presented to Aberlour by James Fleming, a local banker, with £2,000 for its construction.

The **Parish Church** was designed in 1812 to replace St Drostan's, by then *mean and ancient*, with a sensibly enlightened stone box. William Robertson added the stumpy Norman tower, which was the sole survivor of a disastrous fire in 1861. George Petrie rebuilt the church in vigorous Norman style to give the whole building a homogeneity. Some excellent carving on the capitals within. The apse and vestry were added by J. Wittet in 1933 in memory of Sir John Ritchie Findlay. **St Margaret's** uphill in a romantically wooded setting was designed in 1875 by Alexander Ross in sturdy, rubbly, high-roofed Gothic with pretty groups of trefoil windows. All that survives of the celebrated **Orphanage** is the 1889 Clock Tower designed by Alexander Ross. Down by the shore, the 1863 railway has been transformed into the pleasant **Alice Littler Memorial Park,** the pretty pedimented station serving as a tea room.

Top left: The Square. **Top:** The Fleming Institute. **Above:** The Main Street. **Below:** The Alice Littler Park created by the Planning Department from the old railway line.

182 **Aberlour House,** William Robertson, 1838
Two splendid gate lodges facing the road hint at what
lies up the hill: the wonderfully Italianate **East Lodge**
with its oversailing roofs and campanile (1856), and
the handsome Doric temple of the **West Lodge,**
almost certainly designed by Robertson along with the
house.

Alexander Grant, the son of a Glen Rinnes farmer
who made good in Jamaica, purchased the ancestral
seat of the Gordons of Aberlour and commissioned a
great country house on a bluff overlooking the Spey
(the Gordons have the last laugh: it is now the prep
school for Gordonstoun). The design, William
Robertson's masterpiece, is now focused upon a two-
storey *porte-cochère*, very similar to J. B. Papworth's
1839 design for Laleham (Middlesex) and added by
Robertson's nephews A. and W. Reid in 1857. The
upper storey is pedimented and decorated with
anthemion leaves. The house otherwise presented a
large, two storey principal block overlooking tumbling
gardens, with a drawing room wing added in 1890.
The interior contains a splendid staircase and hall,
spacious and cold in its grandeur, and a library
decorated by Sir Robert Lorimer. The estate has good
stables with a prominent bellcote, designed by
Robertson, and gates by Lorimer to the walled garden,
which also has a massive Doric portico. The 60 ft.
high Tuscan **Column,** c. 1834, was re-erected after
collapse by John Ritchie Findlay in 1888, a heraldic
unicorn replacing the original granite ball on top.

183 **Glenallachie Distillery,** Boys Jarvis, 1969-75
This crisp, white-and-black distillery, in its idyllic
setting by the Aberlour Burn, is the most
distinguished of the modern distilleries on Speyside.
The design groups all the parts of the distillery so that
they mass up to the dominant mash house.

Aberlour house: principal facade,
entrance hall, and lodges.

Glenallachie Distillery.

184 Carron

A hill, a daugh, and a railway station — thus in 1892. The railway is no more, transmuted into the **Speyside Way** instead. Note the old bridge over to Carron House with its delicate ironwork. A large industrial township surrounds the 1851 **Dailuaine Distillery,** founded by William Mackenzie in what Alfred Barnard considered to be *one of the most beautiful little glens in Scotland. Never was there such a soft bright landscape of luxuriant green, of clustering foliage, and verdant banks of wild flowers, ferns and grasses.* A distinguishing feature of the distillery is the unreal cragginess of the splayed, crowstepped gables of the bonded stores.

185 Glenfarclas

Without the tall chimney stack, we should have taken it for a scattered farm holding: a compliment by Barnard about how little the distillery disturbs the northern slopes of Ben Rinnes, where it was founded by Robert Hay in 1836. The liquor is excellent, crayfish farming a by-product, the museum interesting and the Visitor's Centre open to the public. The nearby farm of **Marypark,** which gives its name to the adjacent hamlet, grittily crowsteps gables, porch, dormer windows and anything else within reach: the substantial steading behind has a tower above the entrance pend.

Top: Aberlour House column. **Above:** Marypark. **Left:** Carron Bridge over the old railway.

Inveravon: the church and manse are clearly visible.

The lands of Ballindalloch and Glencairnie were granted by King James IV to John Grant of Freuchie on 4th February 1499, for his good and faithful service. Grant's putative son, Patrick, became ancestor of the Ballindalloch branch, his own son John probably beginning the tower. In 1645, Montrose's army plundered and burnt the castle but not, it seems, too drastically. The first Grants of Ballindalloch finally lost their patrimony c. 1711, when the estate was bought by Col. William Grant of the Rothiemurchus branch — a founder of one of the Companies incorporated into the Black Watch. His daughter married into the MacPhersons of Invereshie, from which union the current family of MacPherson-Grant descends.

Inveravon Parish Church.

The River Avon (pronounced A' an) joins the Spey at Ballindalloch ending a spectacularly beautiful run from its source in Loch Avon, on the lower slopes of Ben MacDui. Along its banks, at Inchrory, Delnabo, St Bridget's, Kirkmichael and Drumin, are places of considerable historic interest. Be warned: today, as in 1798, the river can be dangerously deceptive: *a considerable river on a bed chiefly of limestone, and thereby so extremely pellucid as to represent a depth of three feet scarcely equal to one, whereby many have been, to the loss of their lives, deceived.*

186 **Inveravon Parish Church** from 1806
Well worth a detour, if only for its lovely site on a sheltered bluff. The simple harled box is mostly that created by A. Marshall Mackenzie in 1876, but its site is ancient, and the fabric incorporates bits from predecessors. Ballindalloch gallery inside. The old Scots **Mausoleum** to Sir George MacPherson Grant was added by William Robertson in 1829. Pictish stones in the graveyard. The harled **Manse** was recreated in 1834 by William Robertson — pavilion-roofed, porched and pedimented. Worthy 1850 **School** by Thomas Mackenzie on the hill above.

187 **Ballindalloch Castle** from 1542
That this is a fortified house of some originality, rather than a castle, is indicated by its location on a haugh of the Spey, commanded by the bluffs above. Its core is an unusual variant upon the Z-plan: a dominant tower to the south, a three-storey residential block in the middle, and a round, six-storey tower projecting half way along the north. A further, fat stairtower was added, probably in 1718 along with the crow-stepped flanking wings. In 1847, Thomas Mackenzie restored and enlarged it in fashionable style: he heightened the baronial atmosphere, but

mercifully spared much of the original, leaving us with the fairytale dormers, crowsteps, carvings and turrets we have today. A peculiarity is that both round stairtowers are corbelled into the square at the top, and there are small oriel windows (similar to those once found at Balvenie, the Bishop's Palace in Elgin, and at Rothiemay). Mackenzie was also responsible for the Franco-Scots **Lodge** by the water's edge which bears the wonderful motto: *touch not the cat bot a glove.* A large, rectangular, twin-chambered **doocot** is dated 1696.

188 **Kilnmaichlie House,** 17th century
Overlooking the Avon, this venerable mansion was rescued from *the remains of an old Gothic castle of which the tower was almost entire . . . tenanted by kindly daws and swallows* in the mid 18th century by Lady Grant, godmother of Henry Mackenzie (author of **The Man of Feeling**). That probably explains its current appearance of a large principal block, with a projecting three-storey crowstepped tower.

Top: Ballindalloch Castle: drawings for the extension and the gatehouse and a view of the principal tower. **Left:** Kilnmaichlie. **Below:** Drumin Castle.

189 **Drumin Castle,** possibly 14th century
The massive, shattered walls of Drumin still rise to three-storeys, on a bluff above the confluence of the Livet and the Avon. The site's strategic importance guarding the entrance to Speyside from the Lecht is underlined by its possession by Alexander Stewart, Wolf of Badenoch. The nearby **Farm** dates from 1818. The **Silver Bridge** across the Avon at Ballcorach has elegant 19th century bowed trusses. A Pictish **soutterrain** (underground dwelling) and granary survive by the Mains of Inverourie.

GLENLIVET

McKean

Above: Kirkmichael Parish Church.

The Haughs of Cromdale figured in the Glorious Revolution, being the site of the last battle between the supporters of James VII, led by General Buchan, and Government troops under Sir Thomas Livingstone.

The rout of the Jacobites on 1st May 1690 is commemorated in a brisk ballad:

*As I came in by Auchindoun
A little wee bit frae the toun
When to the Highlands I was boun
To view the Haughs of Cromdale,
I met a man in tartan trews
I speirit him — what was the news?
Quo' he — the Heiland army rues
That e'er they came to Cromdale.*

Below: Bridge of Glenlivet.

Moray Planning Dept

190 **Kirkmichael Parish Church,** 1807

The **Market Cross** of this ancient and largely deserted community graces the beautiful kirkyard of Kirkmichael, in whose very walls survives a mediaeval stone fragment. The **Kirk** itself is at least the third on this site, a plain box kirk which owes much of its present state to the now-demolished Free Kirk at Craggan, which was cannibalised to provide materials for rebuilding Kirkmichael after a serious fire in 1951. A curious effigy is to be found above the doorway. At **Bridge of Avon**, the A939 streaks west to Nethy Bridge and Grantown, offering further spectacular, if barren, views of the hills and haughs of Cromdale.

(More details of walks to wells and ancient sites in **Avonside Explored** by Sir Edward Peck.)

191 **GLENLIVET**

Glenlivet presents paradoxes: a Highland area now really part of the Lowlands; remote, yet utterly unlike the Highlands in that it is still populated. It has something of the atmosphere of the Pyrenees: small communities sheltering from great, bleak hills snow-clad till early summer, clear burns, echoes of sheep, brisk wind and a dense sense of history. Acting as its sentinel is the hamlet of **Bridgend of Glenlivet** with its picturesque c. 1800 cottages and double-humped **Bridge.** Picnic site.

The Glenlivet

This neighbourhood wrote Alfred Barnard *has always been famous for its whisky. Formerly, smuggling houses were scattered on every hill, all over the mountain glens, and at that time the smugglers used to lash kegs of spirit on their backs and take them all the way to Aberdeen and Perth for disposal.* That explains the opposition to George Smith of Drumin when he opened the first legal distillery in Glenlivet in 1824; an opposition so

Left: Glenlivet Distillery, Minmore and the hills of Cromdale.

Battle of Glenlivet
The 12 miles of the Livet reek with as much history as distilling. One of the last religious battles in Scotland was fought on its slopes in 1594, by Allt a' Choileachain, just south of the B9009. The Earls of Angus, Huntly and Errol were declared forfeit by the young James VI, on the suspicion of a Catholic conspiracy with the King of Spain. Letters were produced. The young Earl of Argyll was appointed to chastise them, and chose Campbell of Lochnell and Lachlan Maclean of Duart to assist with an army of *10,000 rapacious warriors from the Western Isles and all the coast from Kintyre to Lochaber. Gasping for spoil, they hasten on through Badenoch toward the richer region of Strathbogie:* but were stopped here. Although the Catholics fielded only 1,200 people, they had six small cannon to which the Highlanders were unused. Argyll was defeated, and Maclean of Duart mortally wounded. Legend has it that he asked to be buried where no lowland tongue could be heard, and he may one of the many 720 slain who were buried at Downan.

fierce, that Smith *had to carry firearms for his protection for a long time till they dispersed.* The smugglers were right to be apprehensive: within 20 years, the success of the new distillery had extinguished virtually all other whisky production in the area.

The distillery moved from Upper Drumin to its current site in 1858, and retains of that period the **Manager's House** and a barley loft, now the **Visitors' Centre.** The gables of the bonded warehouses have curious gothic windows flanked by bulls' eyes.

Minmore House Hotel, the farmhouse acquired by George Smith in 1840, is pleasantly old Scots, white-harled, symmetrical, with later bays and wings. **Blairfindy Castle** was built as a hunting seat in 1586 by the Earl of Huntly, and bears a panel with the Gordon arms on its sadly fissured walls. Still impressive (but for how much longer without restoration?), it is L-plan, a wide stair in the wing, hall on first floor as usual, with corbelled turrets at the corners. Was the occupant the hunter or the hunted?

George Smith (1792-1871) a son of the farmer at Upper Drumin, was a local builder and architect until he took over the farm at the death of his father, with its long-established illicit distilling. In 1824, he exploited the 1822 Excise Act to take out a licence for whisky distilling, exporting the spirit through Burghead and Garmouth. He took tack of neighbouring estates to safeguard his barley supply, and took over, for a short while, the distillery at Delnabo. His successors combined distilling with farming and cattle breeding. In 1858 he and his son built a larger distillery at Minmore, the increase in demand being due, in part at least, to the arrival of the railway at Ballindalloch which eased the difficulties of transport.

Left: Glenlivet Distillery.

Right: Tombae. The church can be spotted down by the water's edge.
Above: Blairfindy Castle.

Tombreckachie Mill, now used as a barn, was built c. 1800, like the bridge, and is an attractive L-plan rubble building. At **Auchbreck** a rare Presbyterian outpost in this Catholic enclave was built in 1736, rebuilt to its current form in 1825. By the c. 1800 Aucharachan Farm is a splendid **Standing Stone,** re-erected here, upon its ancestral site, after ill fortune had dogged the farmer who had filched it.

Paul Macpherson (1756-1846) was born at Wester Scalan and trained as a priest (presumably at the seminary on his doorstep). Roman Catholicism still being proscribed in Scotland, his career had to lie in Europe, where he rose to the dignity of Abbé (abbot) and Rector of the Scots College in Rome. During the Napoleonic Wars, agents of the British Government requested his assistance in several difficult diplomatic missions (and, some say, spying). It is said that he agreed on condition that the restrictions upon his religion would be reviewed, relaxed or removed. His efforts were successful and the Government grateful. That demonstration that Catholics were not always traitors is thought to have contributed to the eventual emancipation of the Catholics in 1829, the year Macpherson returned to Scotland to found a church at Scalan. Land was only made available further down the valley at what is now Chapeltown, and here Macpherson established and endowed a church and school. His original priest's house survives (enlarged) as Chapel House.

193 Church of the Incarnation, Tombae, 1829
A chapel under the patronage of the Gordons of Minmore had existed in this neighbourhood, certainly since the early 18th century, on the haugh of the Livet at Kinakyle. It was burnt after the '45, but repaired and used until the Muckle Spate of 1829 scoured away all but the foundations. This delicate box with its pretty gothic windows and finials was designed by the parish priest George Gordon to replace it. The plan is clever, and there is an excellent plaster vaulted interior.

194 Tomnavoulin
A stone and white-harled hillside village with a shop, garage, converted chapel, hedged graveyard and diminutive village green. The huge **Distillery** of the same name, just downhill, has a visitors' centre. Excellent views.

195 Knockandu (or Auchnarrow)
A tiny roadside hamlet with the hospitable and picturesque **Pole Inn,** just by the junction with the route to the Braes of Glenlivet. The graveyard of **Buiternach** just uphill, was consecrated by a priest from Scalan for the Gordons of Minmore, but is now non-denominational: 18th century table-tombs and good 19th century gravestones.

Braes of Glenlivet
The centre of this remote, but fertile bowl is the tiny 196 community of **Chapeltown,** its church and its distillery; but the reason for Chapeltown's very

existence lies a mile up the track at Scalan. The current church of **Our Lady of Perpetual Succour** is the second, designed in 1897 by John Kinross and financed by the Marquess of Bute (the same team that restored the Greyfriars in Elgin). Its tall, crowstepped entrance tower well suited to the encircling fir trees, the church contains an interesting painted ceiling, and a marble slab removed from its predecessor commemorating the founder of this community, the Abbé Paul Macpherson. **Braes of Glenlivet** distillery, 1973, by William Nimmo, is best seen from a distance, where its black and white composition of roofs seems apposite to this wonderful landscape.

Our Lady of Perpetual Succour.

197 **Scalan**

Up a track some distance from Chapeltown is the large, early 18th century farm building which was converted for use as the Roman Catholic College for priests and sons of gentlemen in 1762. The interior is of considerable interest and is open to visitors. The **Muckle Isaac** gives a glimpse of it in use: *The school at present contains from 10 to 12 students under the care of a clergyman who conducts their education and superintends the management of the farm and the house. It is properly the Bishop's seminary for educating a few of the Catholic youth in the principles of grammar and morality, and training them to a regularity of discipline in preparation for the Colleges on the Continent.*

198 The 1844 **Auchriachan Mill,** on the river Conglass, is the sole survivor of four such mills once serving the parish, on a site of some antiquity. Two-storeyed, rubble built, the mill has lost its wheel but kept the threshing barn alongside. James Gordon (1726-1812) farmer at **Croughly,** an 18th century farm with wings further down the river, had the distinction of providing one son and three grandsons who rose to the rank of General. Upstream, **Blairnamarrow,** one of several substantial, early 19th century farmhouses, is said to be on the site of a battle, its gaelic name meaning *Field of the dead.*

Braes of Glenlivet and the view to Scalan.

The College of Scalan
Between 1717 and 1799, over 100 priests were trained illegally at the College of Scalan. Its name probably derives from the gaelic word for turf shieling, *sgalan*. Most of the farms of the lower lands had specific shielings for their herdsmen to overlook the summer grazings, on the hills encircling the Braes. In 1715, the priest at the Castletown of Blairfindy, John Gordon, fled before the troops of General Cadogan and took refuge in one such scalan, beyond the level of normal settlement. Two years later the Catholic seminary at Morar, which had had to close with the defeat of the Jacobites, was re-opened at Scalan, and a stone building was erected for the purpose. By 1746, the College had acquired sufficient notoriety for it to be worth the while of Cumberland's troops to make a long detour to burn it. Repaired, it was eventually abandoned in favour of the farm house opposite in 1762.

167

LECHT

Lecht Iron mine.

In 1730 the York Buildings Company opened an iron mine on this inaccessible spot. Timber being short, the ore had to be carried on horseback, over Fordmouth on the Avon, to Culnakyle, near Nethybridge, where sufficient timber could be had for smelting the ore into *Strathdoun pigs*. The company had a mixed reputation and doubtful track record, and the mine closed in 1737. It was re-opened in 1841 by Donald Smith on behalf of the Duke of Gordon, with the installation of a crushing mill, and construction of a mill lade. The mill wheels, which came from Aberdeen, were enormous, and the bull belonging to the Minister of Corgarff was pressed into service to assist the horses tow their load up the Lecht. A shaft 85 ft. deep was sunk, and at its peak the mine employed 63 people extracting manganese, which was exported through Portgordon. Unfortunately, cheap imports of manganese from Russia ruined its economics, and the mine closed finally in 1846.

The ruined cottage about half a mile beyond Blairnamarrow is that in which the *Monocled Mutineer* Percy Toplis hid when on the run, under suspicion of murder of a taxi driver near Aldershot in June 1920. He attracted attention by stripping the woodwork to make a fire, and shot and wounded two of those who came to enquire the score. Five days later he was killed near Penrith.

33rd Regiment Memorial.

THE LECHT

An ancient pass guarded at the north by Drumin Castle and at the south by the notorious Corgarff; and the first road in Scotland likely to be closed by snow. The road was built in 1754 by soldiers of the 33rd Regiment under Lord Charles Hay, who left a carved 199**Memorial** at the Well of Lecht. The former **Iron Mine** was probably built by the York Buildings Company in 1730 as part of their exploitation of forfeited Jacobite estates. Recently restored by the District Council, with a pleasant picnic spot nearby, the Mill is a square, two-storeyed building built of locally quarried quartzite, characterised by a large archway on the ground floor.

The developments relating to skiing are — as elsewhere in Scotland — a wasted opportunity.

200 TOMINTOUL

A brisk place, which feels as though it is on the roof of Scotland; and thus appropriate for the outdoor sportsmen, tourists and, latterly, skiers who have provided the money for it to rise above the *tumbledown, miserable, dirty-looking place* that Queen Victoria recorded in 1853. It is well supplied with shops and hotels and there is an excellent museum facing the Square.

The Gaelic name probably means *barn knoll*, for there was always a hamlet of some sort on the rise to the south west of the town. In 1775, the improving Duke of Gordon decided to provide a focus for the several sizeable communities that lay scattered in this remote hinterland (and which were undoubtedly offering succour to the reivers and cattle lifters). Thus, on this *improveable bog* he founded a town *in a regular manner so as the Publick Road may be the high Street* with a *right Publick house for the accomodation of travailers and others . . . built in the most centrical part of the Town.* The first of the *tennements to be built in a regular manner, all fronting the street of equal height and*

McKean

as *uniform as possible* were completed in 1780. The concentration upon this new town inevitably led to a decline in the surrounding parts: to it came the Inn from Camdelmore, the market from Minmore, the school from Tomachlaggan, and many of the people. In 1826, the new Church began to replace the ancient kirk at Kirkmichael.

The 40 ft. width of the street and 90,000 sq. ft. of the Square is somewhat too spacious to control the wind, and it is in the back lanes and narrower parts that the charm of Tomintoul may better be appreciated.

The Church, 1826, Thomas Telford
Designed originally as a Parliamentary Church (one erected after an Act of Parliament had identified serious shortages), it was given its pretty Gothic dress of buttresses, belltower and finial by John Robertson in 1900. The elegant winged **Manse** could also be Telford's design. The 1837 **Catholic Chapel** in Tomnabat Lane is considerably more exotic, in keeping with the flamboyance shown in Presholme, Keith and Tombae: a harled, gabled entrance tower and pedimented doorway.

The Square contains some desultory trees, a 1915 fountain, much breeze, the **Museum** with its reconstructed kitchen and blacksmith's shop, and the hotels. Of these, the dominant is the **Richmond Arms,** 1858, a solid, three-storey corner building of regular windows and wall head gables. The **Gordon Arms,** rebuilt c. 1900, has less swagger, although there are two storeys in the roof. The **Main Street** is lined with stone or harled cottages, some c. 1810, and others gable-end to the street in defiance of the original feu. Most bear roof extensions from the days of Victorian expansion, some with ranks of pedimented and finialled dormer windows. Facing up

Above: Tomintoul from the Square.

The Duke's intention that the community should become self-supporting with a lint mill, weaving, a bleach field and quarries, proved over-optimistic. In 1798, only 37 families were living there — using barely over half the feus available, and there was no manufacture: *only some necessary articles of merchandise retailed.* It has been the tourists, from Victoria's visit onwards, who have provided Tomintoul with its purpose.

Below: The Catholic Chapel, Tomnabat Lane.

McKean

Above: Richmond Hall.

The whisky range available from some of Tomintoul's shops is staggering, as would be the state of its consumers, were they wishing to taste a broad sample. The First Statistical Account reveals a long tradition of that kind of thing in Tomintoul: *All of them sell whisky, and all of them drink it. When disengaged on this business, the women spin yarn, kiss their inameratos, or dance to the discordant sounds of an old fiddle. The men, when not participating in the amusements of women, sell small articles of merchandise or let themselves occasionally for a day's labour.*

Below: Delnabo. **Below right:** Inchrory Lodge.

from Tomnabat Lane is the pedimented Venetian window of the **Richmond Hall,** rebuilt as a Memorial Hall and Library after the First World War.

A track leads west from Tomnabat Lane down to the slopes of the Avon and the 18th century farm of **St Bridget,** more celebrated for its connections than its content. Here retired John Gordon of Glenbuchat in 1742, at the age of 68. This prominent Jacobite (known to his enemies as "Auld Glenbucket") held the office of Principal Bailie of the area for the Gordons of Huntly. In 1745 he raised a regiment for Prince Charlie, and came to hide here after Culloden. He witnessed his house being burnt by Cumberland's troops prior to his final exile to France. The farm was rebuilt soon afterwards.

Upper Strathavon offers superb scenery. **Delnabo** is a place of some antiquity although the current building, with its turret, dates from the early 19th century. In the 17th century, it was the haunt of part of the proscribed MacGregor clan (see **Stirling and the Trossachs** volume) the chief, Gregor Macgregor, living here with members of the Glenstrae sept after marrying Margaret Sinclair, widow of Grant of Carron. It was at Delnabo that the 2nd Marquis of Huntly was captured in 1647, to be executed two years later.

Inchrory Lodge, beyond the Burn of the Little Fergie, is a plain, 1847, white hunting lodge, now the centre of a great estate. In 1747, however, it was the site of a military patrol against the cattle reivers, whose main route from the rich lands of Banff and Aberdeenshire back to their fastnesses was through Glen Avon and Glen Loin.

ACKNOWLEDGEMENTS

Particular thanks are due to Elizabeth Beaton to whom much of the original research is due. I am indebted considerably to Mike Seton (and his many publications), Robert Stewart and his staff in the District Planning Department, John Knight, N. V. R. Simpson, S. A. Mitchell, Bruce Walker, Judith Scott, George Campbell, Ian Keillar, Ian Smith, Douglas Forrest, Andrew Wright and family, Ray Marshall, Alistair Murdoch, John Loud, Miss E. Rhynas, George Ripley, Les Brown, Ian Shepherd, Ian Gow and the staff of the Royal Commission on the Ancient and Historical Monuments of Scotland, and Stewart McBain of Messrs Chivas Ltd. Joyce Lawrie and Tayona McKeown did much of the typing.

PHOTOGRAPHIC CREDITS
As is normal in this series, the photographer or the source of the photograph is credited alongside each. In general, considerable thanks must go, again, to the RCAHMS, the Moray District Department of Physical Planning, Douglas Forrest and his office, the architects who supplied photographs, Andrew Wright, Mike Seton and the collection in Elgin Library, Tony Gorzgowski, Alan Jeffrey (for the loan of his camera) and Chivas Brothers Ltd. White House Photography produced superlative development work, Councillor Mrs Jennifer Shaw, Colonel and Mrs Black of Leuchars, the Duke of Buccleuch, Woodmansterne Ltd., the Abbot Sancta Maria Abbey, Nunraw, I. O. Morison, Moray District Department of Libraries.

The assistance of Moray District Council, Messrs Chivas Brothers Ltd. a subsidiary of the Seagram Co., Canada, and the Highlands and Islands Development Board made this project possible and their help is gratefully acknowledged.

REFERENCES
As is normal in this series, the usual method of reference is impossible. **The Pageant of Morayland**, J. B. Ritchie, 1953; **Tomintoul, its glens and its people**, Victor Gaffney, 1970; **The Whisky Distilleries of Scotland**, Alfred Barnard, 1887; **Strathisla:** 200 years of distilling tradition, Stewart McBain; **Moray Firth**, by Cuthbert Graham; **Scottish Ballad Poetry**, ed. by George Eyre-Todd; **Songs of Scotland**, G. F. Graham, 1845; **The Gazetteer of Scotland**, 1842; **Ordnance Gazetteer of Scotland**, Francis Groome, 1892; **Beauties of Scotland**, Forsyth, 1805; **Morayshire Described**, J. & W. Watson, 1868; **Tour of Scotland**, Thomas Pennant, 1772; **Letters to Thomas Pennant**, 1776, Charles Cordiner; **Remarkable Ruins**, Charles Cordiner; **Scotland Illustrated**, William Beattie (1837); **Baronial and Ecclesiastical Antiquities of Scotland**; R. W. Billings, 1846-1852; **Diary**, Queen Victoria; **The Annals of Cullen**, W. Crammond; **Avonside Explored**, Sir Edward Peck; **The Whisky Roads of Scotland**, Derek Cooper and Fay Godwin; **Industrial Archaeology of Scotland**, John Hume; **Speyside Past and Present**, Mike Seton; **Distilleries of Moray**, Mike Seton; **Churches of Moray**, Angus Mowat and Mike Seton; **Moray Past and Present**, Mike Seton; **Laich o' Moray**, Mike Seton; **Forres Past and Present**, Mike Seton; **Elgin Past and Present**, Mike Seton (pub. Moray District Libraries); **Cathedrals, Abbeys and Priories in Moray**, Ian Keillar (Moray Field Club); **Pencillings by the Way**, Nathaniel Willis, 1836; **Circuit Journeys**, Lord Cockburn; **Survey of the Province of Moray**, 1798 (Isaac Forsyth); **Theatrum Scotia**, Captain John Slezer, 1692; **The Castellated and Domestic Architecture of Scotland**, David MacGibbon and Thomas Ross, 1897; **The Ecclesiastical Architecture of Scotland**, David MacGibbon and Thomas Ross, 1897; **Antiquities of Scotland**, Captain Francis Grose, 1797; **Grampian — Exploring Scotland's Heritage**, Ian Shepherd (HMSO, 1986); **Moray Antiquities**, D. Alexander, 1843; **Doocots of Moray**, Elizabeth Beaton (Moray Field Club); **Architecture of Morayshire**, Ian Gow (Architectural Heritage Society of Scotland); **The Rulers of Strathspey**, Earl of Cassillis, 1911; **Journal of a Tour to the North of Scotland**, Alexander Carlyle, 1765; **Elgin Past and Present**, H. B. Mackintosh; **Prehistoric Scotland**, Richard Feachem; **The Landscape Garden in Scotland**, A. A. Tait; **The Lintie o' Moray**, William Hay; **Scottish Pioneers of the Greek Revival**, Scottish Georgian Society; **Tour Through the Whole Island of Great Britain**, Daniel Defoe; **New Ways Through the Glens**, A. R. B. Haldane; **Early Travellers in Scotland**, Hume Brown; **Beyond the Highland Line**, A. J. Youngson; **History of Scotland**, George Buchanan; **The Moray Book**, ed. D. Omand (Harris, 1976).

About the year 1730, the York Buildings Company purchased the timber of the woods of Abernethy to the amount of nearly £7,000 sterling. Great indeed was their beginning: every kind of implement of the best form, 120 work-horses, wagons, elegant wooden houses, saw-mills, and an iron-foundry, all surprising novelties in the country. Besides the saw-mills which they constructed, and the roads which they formed through the woods, Mr Aaron Hill the poet, the clerk of this establishment, first showed the mode of binding three or four score of spars together into a platform . . . and navigated down the river by a man seated at each end with an oar. . . . Tradition relates that the establishment were the most extravagant set ever known in the country, that their wasteful prodigality ruined themselves and in part corrupted others. Their profusion was frequently displayed in bonfires of whole barrels of tar; and entire hogsheads of brandy were broached among the people by which five men, in one night, died. The York Buildings Company had been established to exploit forfeited Jacobite estates, and since their asset — stripping of the Speyside hills was unpopular, the above story should be treated with reserve.

Aerial Photography has revealed that the Pass of Grange contained two Roman marching forts: a small, 25 acre camp on the banks of the Isla at Auchinhove, and a much larger one at Muiryfold just to the east, with a roadway over Sillyearn Hill. Although both may be 3rd century erections attributed to the campaign of Severus, it has also been suggested that they might indicate an earlier presence; and, in particular, the proximity of the famous battle site of **Mons Graupius** in which (so Tacitus recorded) Agricola and the Romans inflicted a serious defeat on the local Pictish tribes in A.D. 84.

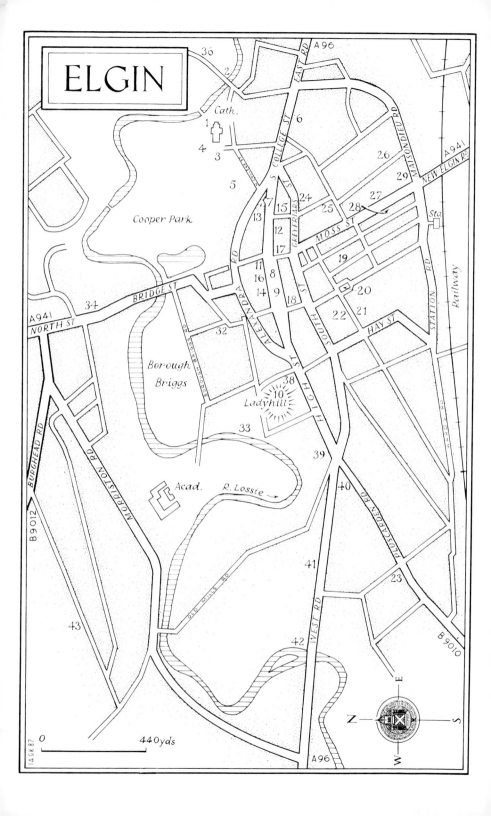

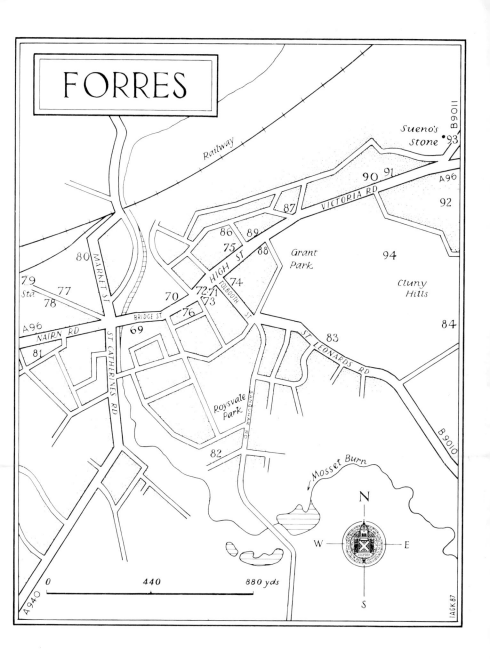

FORRES

Railway

Sueno's Stone •93

B9011

A96

90 91

VICTORIA RD

92

87

86 89

75

HIGH ST

88

Grant Park

94

80

MARKET ST

74

Cluny Hills

79

Sta

77

70

72 71

73

TOLBOOTH ST

84

78

BRIDGE ST

76

A96

NAIRN RD

69

ST CATHERINS RD

ST LEONARDS RD

83

81

Roysvale Park

SANCHAR RD

B9010

82

Mosset Burn

N

W   E

S

A940

0   440   880 yds

IACK 87

INDEX

A

Aberlour House, 160-1
Aberlour (Charlestown of), 158-60
Abernethy, James, 158
Adam, James, 134-5
Adam, John, 57
Adam, Robert, 124
Adam, William, 23, 131, 134-5
Aldivalloch, 151
Altyre, 53-4
Alves, Crook of, 82-3
Archiestown, 155-6
Arndilly, 154
Asliesk Castle, 83
Auchindoun, 150-1
Auchinroath, 154
Auchlunkart, 144
Auchriachan, 167
Auchroisk, 144
Avon, River, 162*ff*
Aytoun, William, 106

B

Ballindalloch Castle, 163
Balvenie Castle, 146-8
Barnett, P. M., 30, 130
Bartlam Ashley Partnership, 23, 24, 51
Baxter, John, 114, 116-7
Birnie Kirk, 64
Bishopmill, 41-2
Blairnamarrow, 167
Blairfindy Castle, 165
Blervie Castle and House, 61
Boat of Brig, 152
Boharm, 144-5
Boswell, James, 8, 22, 116, 128
Botriphnie, 145
Boys Jarvis, 160
Braes of Glenlivet, 166
Brodie, 54-6, 84
Bryce, David, 135
Buckie, 92, 121-3
Buchromb, 146
Burghead, 86-7, 90
Burgie Castle, 83
Burn, William, 25, 55
Burnet, Sir John, 102
Bute, Marquess (and family) of, 35, 62, 167

C

Cabrach, The, 151
Cairnfield House, 124
Cardow, 156
Carron, 161
Carruthers, W. L., 53-4, 60
Cattanach, Col. Alec, 30, 102
Chalmers, P. MacGregor, 37
Churches:
  Bellie Church, Fochabers, 117
  Chinese Church, Elgin, 43
  Cullen, Old Kirk, 132
  Free Church, Elgin, 31
  Grange Kirk, 136
  High United Free, Elgin, 31
  Holy Trinity, Elgin, 40
  Kirkmichael, 164
  Michael Kirk, Gordonstoun, 98-9
  North Parish Church, Buckie, 121
  Our Lady of Perpetual Succour, Chapeltown, 167
  Muckle Kirk, Elgin, 20
  Presholme, 124

  South Church, Elgin, 32
  Speymouth Kirk, 111
  St Andrew's, Llanbryde, 108
  St Columba's, Elgin, 20, 37
  St Drostan's, Aberlour, 158
  St Gerardine's, Lossiemouth, 101-2
  St Giles', Elgin, 21-2
  St John's, Forres, 74
  St Laurence, Forres, 66
  St Leonard's, Forres, 70
  St Margaret's, Forres, 74
  St Ninian's, Tynet, 120
  St Peter's, Buckie, 122
  St Rufus', Keith, 140
  St Sylvester's, Elgin, 37
  St Thomas', Keith, 143
Cockburn, Lord, 15, 54, 68, 117
Comyn family, 49, 50-1, 53, 59
Cousin, David, 25
Covesea, 100
Coxton, 2, 110
Craigellachie, 157
Croughly, 167
Culbin Sands, 56-7, 59
Cullen, 93, 128-136
Cummingston, 90

D

Dallas, 59-61
Dalvey, 54, 58
Darnaway, 51-3
Deas, Frank, 61
Defoe, Daniel, 8
Delnabo, 170
Deskford, 136
Dipple, 152
Doig, Charles (Jun.), 17
Doig, Charles (Sen.), 37, 154, 157
Drumin Castle, 163
Drummuir, 145-6
Duff family of Keithmore, Dipple and Braco, 23, 64, 139, 147-8
Duffus Castle, Kirk, New Duffus, 85, 91, 94, 95
Duke of York Tower, 83
Duncan, D. and A., 50-1
Dunphail, 50-1
Dufftown, 149-50
Dyke, 56

E

Edingight, 137
Edinkillie, 49
Elchies, Easter, 155
Elgin Cathedral, 7, 10-15, 81
  Bishop's Palace, 14-15
  Pann's Port, 14
  Unthank Manse, 14
  North College, 14-16
Elgin:
  Academy Street and Academy, 31-33
  Anderson's Institution, 17
  Arcades, 8, 22-4
  Alexandra Road, 9, 40
  Bield, The, 48
  Bow Bridge, 48
  Braco's Banking House, 23-4
  Braelossie, 47-8
  Castle Hill, 22
  Chanonry, 9, 14-15
  Closes, 24-26
  Clydesdale Bank, 28
  Cooper Park, 14, 16
  Commerce Street, 27-8

  Courthouse, 26
  Duff Avenue, 37
  Duke of Gordon Monument, 22
  Elgin Club, 28
  Elgin Motors, 17
  Gaol, 20
  Grant Lodge, 16
  Grays Hospital, 46
  Grant Street, 34, 45
  Greyfriars, 34-5
  Hamilton Drive, 48
  Harrison Terrace, 43
  Hay Street, 33-4
  The Haugh, 40
  Highfield, 30
  High Street, 8, 9, 20-27
  Institution Road, 35-6
  Little Cross, 7, 8, 18
  Muckle Cross, 19, 21
  King Street, 14-16
  Ladyhill and House, 45
  Laich Moray Hotel, 38
  Lesmurdie, 43
  Lossie Green, 41
  Maisondieu, 34-5
  Maryhill, 45
  Moray Street, 32-3
  Muckle Kirk, 20
  Murdoch's Wynd, 44
  Museum, 18
  New Market, 30
  Newmill, 43
  North Street, 9, 40
  North College Street, 18
  Old Mills, 48
  Playhouse, 28
  Reidhaven Street, Elgin, 31-2
  Royal Bank, 25
  Shepherd's Close, 23
  Sheriff Court, 26
  Sheriffmill Bridge, 48
  South College Street, 17
  South Guildry Street, 31-2
  South Street, 30-1
  South Villa, 38
  Station, 38
  Thunderton House, 29-30
  Town Hall, 32
  Tower, 22
  Union Buildings, 27
  Victoria School, 33
  West Road, 47-8
Ellis, Alexander, 122
Enzie, The, 120

F

Findhorn, 78-80, 85
Findhorn Foundation, 80
Findochty, 92, 125-6
Findrassie, 105
Fochabers, 114, 116-119
Forres: 12, 20, 65-76, 86
  Academy, 72
  Anderson's School, 74
  Bank of Scotland, 70
  Cattle Mart, 70-1
  Cluny, 75
  Cluny Hill College, 73
  Culbin Stores, 70
  Drumduan, 76
  Falconer Museum, 69
  High Street, 66-70
  Leanchoil Hospital, 73
  Nelson's Tower, 76
  North Road, 73-4

Park Hotel, 75
Ramnee Hotel, 75
Royal Hotel, 70
St Leonard's Road, 73
Station, 70-1
Tolbooth, 66
Town Hall, 69
Victoria Hotel, 70
Victoria Road, 74-5
Forrest, Douglas, 134
Forsyth, Isaac, 22
Fulton, Peter, 66, 70

G

Garmouth, 88, 111-2
Gibbs, James, 23, 147-8
Glenallachie Distillery, 160-1
Glenfarclas, 161
Glenfiddich, 148
Glenlivet, 164-5
Goodwillie, Thomas, 22
Gordon Castle, 114-5
Gordon, Edom o', 150-1
Gordonstoun, 95, 97-9
Graham, James Gillespie, 46, 47, 61, 77, 108
Grange Hall, 58-9
Greshop, 58

H

Hazelwood, 146
Heiton, Andrew, 27
Hopeman, 90
Hughes, Patrick, 95
Hurd, Robert, and Partners, 56

I

Inchbroom, 106
Inchgower, 123
Inchrory, 170
Innes, Cosmo, 9
Innes House, 106-7
Inveravon, 162
Invererne, 58
Inverugie, 90

J

Johnson, Dr Sam, 8, 12, 67, 128

K

Keith, 139-144
Kellas, 61
Kennedy, G. R. M., 33, 37, 73, 76, 101
Kidner, William, 40-1, 43-4
Kilnmaichlie, 163
Kincorth, 57-8
Kingston, 88, 112
Kininmonth and Spence, 41
Kininvie, 146
Kinloss Abbey, 76-8
Kinneddar, 100
Kinross, John, 35, 53, 54, 167
Knockando, 156
Knockandu, 166
Knockomie, 54

L

Laing, Alexander, 53
Laird, Michael, 155
Law and Dunbar Nasmith, 51, 62 68, 72
Lecht, The, 168
Letterfourie, 124
Leuchars, 106
Lindsay, Ian G., 120

Llanbryde, 109
Lochindorb, 49
Logie, 51
Longhill Mill, 108
Lorimer, Sir Robert, 107, 160
Lossiemouth, 88, 100-3

M

Macallan, 155
MacDonald, Alister, 28
MacDonald, Ramsay, 102-3
McGill, Alexander, 134
Mackenzie, A. Marshall, 16, 19, 32-3, 44-5, 47, 64, 102, 107, 162
Mackenzie, Henry, 163
Mackenzie, Thomas, 18, 19, 36, 38, 44-5, 68, 74, 109, 118, 145, 149, 154, 162, 163
Mackenzie and Cruikshank, 70
Mackenzie, William, 161
MacPherson, Abbé Paul, 166
MacMillan, Duncan, 121, 130
MacWilliam, George, 101-2, 128
Maggieknockater, 145
Matthews, James, 129, 158
Marypark, 161
Mayen, 138
Milne's High School, Fochabers, 118
Minmore, 165
Milton Brodie, 80, 82
Milton Duff, 64
Milton Tower, Keith, 140
Mitchell, Sydney, 19
Moray District Architects Dept., 44
Mortlach, 148-9
Mosstodloch, 112-3
Moy, 57
Mulben, 144

N

New Elgin, 39
Newmill, 144
Newton House, 83
Nimmo, William, 151, 167

O

Oakwood Motel, 82
Orton House, 152

P

Peddie, J. M. Dick, 161
Peddie and Kinnear, 25
Petrie, George, 70, 159
Pitgaveny, 106
Playfair, James, 135
Playfair, William, 50
Pluscarden Abbey, 62-4, 84
Portessie, 123
Portgordon, 120
Portknockie, 126-7
Portsmouth, Percy, 19
Pratt, R. B., 27
Presholme, 124
Pugin, P. P., 124

Q

Quarrywood House, 105

R

Rafford, 61
Randolph's Leap, 50
Rannas, 124
Rathven, 123

Reiach and Hall, 46, 72
Reid, A. and W., 24, 26, 32, 36-7, 45, 48, 53, 62, 69, 70, 90-1, 100, 141, 159, 160
Relugas, 50
Ripley, George, 80
Robertson, F. D., 141
Robertson, John, 66, 169
Robertson, William, 26, 34, 38, 66, 68, 74, 80, 82, 107, 127, 128-31, 152, 159, 160, 164
Rodney's Stone, 56
Ross, Alexander, 122, 143, 150, 154, 159
Rothes, 153-4
Rothiemay, 137-8
Roumieux, Abraham, 114

S

Scalan, 167
Seafield, Earls of, 16, 128, 133-5
Sea Park, 80
Shanks, John, 15
Sheriffston, 108
Silver Bridge, 163
Simpson, Archibald, 21, 36, 68, 113, 116, 118, 146
Sluie Cottages, 54
Smith, George, of Drumin, 164-5
Smith, James, 135
Southey, Robert, 8, 58, 136, 153
Spey Bay, 119
Spey Bridge, 113
Speymouth, 110-11
Spynie Palace, 101, 104-5
St Bridget, 170
Stark, William, 59
Stewart, Charles, 75-6
Strathisla Distillery, 140
Stynie, 111
Sueno's Stone, 75-6
Sutherland, George, 33

T

Telford, Thomas, 105, 113, 157, 169
Thornybank, 124
Tolbooths:
    Elgin, 7, 20
    Forres, 66
Tombae, 166
Tomintoul, 168-70
Tomnavoulin, 166
Tor Castle, 59
Troup, F. W., 103
Tugnet Ice House, 119
Tynet, 120

U

Urquhart, 108-9

W

Walkerdales, 124
Wardrop, Maitland, 53
Westertown, 62
Willet, John, 138
Williamson, Colen, 57
Wilson, Patrick, 74
Wittet, J. and W., (Wittets Ltd.), 34, 43, 74, 102, 103, 159
Wittet Drive, 34
Woodroffe, W. H., 54
Wright, John, 39, 43
Wylson, James, 55

Y

Yardie, 122

PICTORIAL GLOSSARY

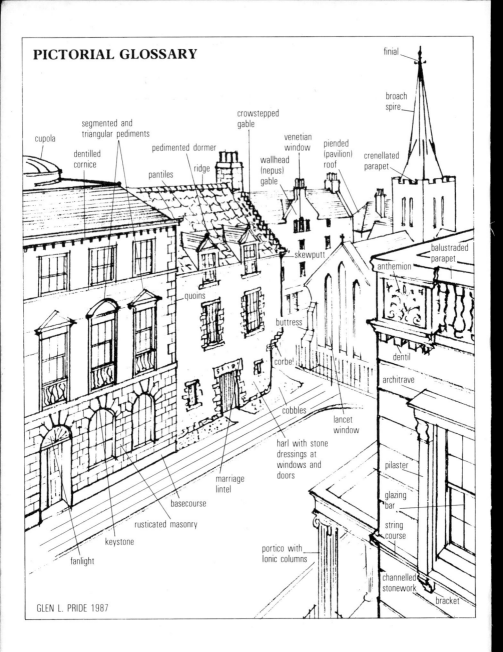

finial

broach spire

crowstepped gable

segmented and triangular pediments

cupola

dentilled cornice

pedimented dormer

pantiles

ridge

venetian window

wallhead (nepus) gable

piended (pavilion) roof

crenellated parapet

balustraded parapet

anthemion

skewputt

quoins

buttress

corbel

cobbles

lancet window

dentil

architrave

harl with stone dressings at windows and doors

pilaster

glazing bar

string course

marriage lintel

basecourse

rusticated masonry

keystone

fanlight

portico with Ionic columns

channelled stonework

bracket

GLEN L. PRIDE 1987